Research and Profit Maximization in Finance and Economics

Christopher E. S. Warburton

University Press of America,® Inc.
Lanham · Boulder · New York · Toronto · Oxford

4501 Forbes Boulevard
Suite 200
Lanham, Maryland 20706
UPA Acquisitions Department (301) 459-3366

PO Box 317
Oxford
OX2 9RU, UK

Printed in the United States of America
British Library Cataloging in Publication Information Available

Library of Congress Control Number: 2005935691
ISBN-13: 978-0-7618-3382-6 (paperback : alk. paper)
ISBN-10: 0-7618-3382-X (paperback : alk. paper)

The paper used in this publication meets the minimum requirements of American National Standard for Information Sciences—Permanence of Paper for Printed Library Materials, ANSI Z39.48—1984

To

Dominick Salvatore, Ziggy MacDonald, and Paul Turner

Contents

Introduction

This work is intended to guide young researchers in the field of Finance and Economics to enable them to do research and use the tools of forecasting and linear programming in business operation. Consequently it has been made deliberately simple and structured to accommodate the apprehensions of neophytes or young researchers who are normally worried about data collection, data estimation, and inferences. The objective of this book is therefore a practical one which puts the subject matter of research and inference in the hands of the reader and encourages the reader to embark on a meaningful research process aided by practical examples without being overwhelmed by theory.

The motives for undertaking a research are addressed in chapter 1. Motives for research are not entirely diverse. They are normally geared toward the acquisition of information to make policy or satisfy an academic criterion; increase income; or provide a remedy to real or perceived problems. While dire necessity might compel inquiry or research, research may not be altogether exciting to those who do not consider it to be imperative. When it is made to be imperative, it sometimes becomes a daunting task to the neophyte who is immediately overwhelmed by thoughts about how to proceed.

Attaining these goals requires a method or conventional methodology. The methodology is also discussed in chapter 1. The procedure of undertaking research could best be perceived of as a process which starts with the selection of a topic and the acquisition of data; neither of which is easy. The issue of sample size is not normally given prompt attention but is also an integral component of the formative stage. In actual fact it goes *in tandem* with data collection.

Samples represent a population of interest and therefore must be large enough to make relevant statistical or economic inferences. Samples are useful or practical because it is normally impractical or improbable to access the complete set of objects that the researcher is interested in. Largeness of course subsumes a probability distribution which is based on the *Law of Averages*—the theory that if a sample is random and large enough, the probability distribution of variables in such a sample, on average, will approximate the true/expected value of the random variables as the number of observations increase.

The selection of a sample type is largely contingent on the research objective. Although the objectives may vary the consequences of biased/prejudicial or flawed samples do not. Flawed samples provide adverse and misleading results which are bad for inferences. It is therefore a good idea to avoid bad samples; for example, samples of convenience which consider some information but concurrently exclude valuable information.

The types of data normally encountered in the research process are briefly discussed in chapter 1. Depending on the type of research, data selection could be one of three types: (i) cross section; (ii) time series; and (iii) pooled. Data are, simply put, information to be estimated. Time series data show a chronological sequence of observations usually in numerical form. Cross section data are data on one or more variables collected at the same time. A special type of cross section data is micropanel data in which a cross section unit is observed over a period of time. This work is primarily concerned with time series analysis although slight and indirect references are made to cross-sectional analysis under "estimation". Estimation is treated as a crucial prelude to inference.

Advances in Econometrics have now given researchers the opportunity to diversify their estimation skills in order to arrive at the best estimate of the data. Estimation of course is closely related to the type of variables to be dealt with and the financial or economic theory to be evaluated or espoused. For example, variables like wealth and income which are interdependent or indicate dual causality create a simultaneity or co-linearity problem depending on the nature of the specification (i.e.) the dependent and independent variables of choice. If both are explanatory variables the researcher would have to deal with a co-linearity problem. If one is a dependent variable, the researcher would have to deal with a dual causality (simultaneity) problem. Fortunately these kinds of problems could be minimized by choosing an estimation method (instrumental variable or two-stage least squares) to deal with the causality problem, conducting tests, and choosing the right kinds of variables. Some statistical or econometric packages make this an easy undertaking. Problems associated with estimation are discussed in the chapter.

The post-estimation analysis is what really makes the research meaningful. At the end of a tedious process the researcher would like to know whether his findings are meaningful or significant. It is assumed that the driving force behind the research is to influence policy, increase income, or deal with a problem or potential problem. The objective therefore necessitates an informative conclusion or outcome of the research process. This is the essence of inference from the estimation of data. The importance of inference is discussed in the light of variable, coefficient and hypothesis tests.

Obtaining data is seldom an easy endeavor. The content of chapter two is intended to minimize the challenge and the pain of identifying data sources. The chapter is designed to lead young researchers to sources of information. It should be immediately pointed out that these sources are not exhaustive, but very helpful to identifying credible sources of information and sources from which information on prominent variables in Finance and Economics could be obtained. It is trite to state that it is impossible to cover all sources, good and bad.

The sources have been selected for their wide appeal and transparency to researchers in the field of Finance and Economics quite apart from their longevity. They cover diverse variables: interest rates; employment; inflation; national output; stock prices; volume of financial assets traded; exchange rates; money supply; population; consumption; savings; consumer confidence; international trade; and corruption. In actual fact the list is just an example of the amount of information that could be obtained; an innumerable amount of information is unlisted.

A brief history is provided of the various sources to give the researcher some amount of background information of the institutions or organizations, and to some extent, the way they collect their data. More information is readily available from the listed sources. The sources include: The New York Stock Exchange; The Federal Reserve Board; Bureau of Labor Statistics; Bureau of Economic Analysis; Bureau of Census; Chicago Board of Trade; National Association of Securities Dealers Automated Quotation System; American Stock Exchange; Yahoo Finance; University of Michigan's Consumer Sentiment Index; World Bank; International Monetary Fund; and Transparency International.

One of the central objectives of this work is to make research meaningful, easy, and practical. The last two chapters of the book are dedicated to those objectives. In chapter 4 the science and art of forecasting is dealt with in an evolutionary step by step process to help the neophyte forecaster. The approach to forecasting in the chapter is conservative and prudent. A method is used which allows the forecaster to first evaluate his forecast by using known information to evaluate his forecast, and calibrate his results before making projections. In this chapter the reader is reminded that forecasting is an intelligent projection based on all available information. In actual fact the soothsaying abilities of a preponderant number of normal humans are exceedingly limited.

Forecasting is discussed at two levels: (i) forecasting which is preliminary and does not necessarily require the data to be stationary; and (ii) atheoretic forecasting using the Box-Jenkins approach, which requires stationarity of the data. The reader is introduced to the various forms of forecasting with nonstationary data. The key concepts which are discussed include: the secular trend; seasonality; and irregular (episodic) variation.

Because forecasting is closely intertwined with the typical regression analysis, regression analysis is discussed briefly. The three major forecasting options are discussed in the light of regression analysis. These include: (i) univariate forecasting, which requires the use of only one variable and is premised on past observances of data on that variable; (ii) bivariate forecasting, which requires forecasting based on the use of two variables; and (iii) multivariate forecasting which requires the use of three or more variables. In each case complete examples are given which are intended to guide the reader to make independent forecasts.

The Box-Jenkins (BJ) methodology as discussed is a special class of univariate forecasting which requires the data to be stationary. Stationarity requires a constant mean, variance, and covariance. The presentation in the chapter deals with all the stages of BJ methodology. Each stage is fully exemplified by the use of real data and variables. The preliminary objective is identified as an approach to identify the data generating process for forecasting so as to determine an appropriate model; namely: an autoregressive (AR); moving average (MA); or integrated model or autoregressive integrated moving average (ARIMA) model. The discussions and examples, including correlograms, are centered on: identification; estimation; diagnostic checking; and forecasting.

The book concludes with a chapter on constrained optimization which is integral to decisions on the use of scarce resources to minimize cost or maximize profit. The last two chapters are interrelated, and important to almost all if not all financial operations of contemporary businesses. Four approaches and their suitability of usage to economic conditions are discussed. These are: (i) multivariate optimization; (ii) Lagrangian optimization; (iii) graphing; and (iv) Excel spreadsheet. The inclusion of the spreadsheet is an attempt to modernize the use of constrained optimization using contemporary technology, but also to allow the reader to be conversant with a method that is more flexible and capable of handling diverse decision variables. The use of Excel and guidance to using Excel for the purpose of optimization is discussed.

Research and Profit Maximization in Finance and Economics is a tool for ambitious young researchers and businesses interested in gaining a comprehensive insight into how to do research and apply forecasting and constrained optimization techniques (linear programming) to economic problems. It provides an opportunity for the reader to develop the skills required for research while at the same time using available technology to accomplish that goal. The questions at the end of each chapter are specifically designed toward that end. Therefore its emphasis sets it aside from traditional texts to put it squarely in the realm of what is practical and immediately useful to students and professionals who are interested in making a breakthrough in the areas of research, forecasting and linear programming. It is hoped that at the end the reader would be able to achieve complete confidence and independence in meeting subsequent challenges in the areas of research, forecasting, and linear programming.

CHAPTER 1

WHY RESEARCH?

Research is a systematic inquiry or investigation to establish facts. While hypotheses (unproven but testable statements/assertions) could be disputed, facts could not. There are significant reasons for facts to be established in various disciplines. Facts become a basis for making policies sensibly. However, disciplines which are involved with the study of human behavior, normally called social sciences, generally have a hard time coming up with universal facts of human behavior because of the fact that human beings are complex and they do not readily lend themselves to *a-priori* conclusions. Because of this difficulty, the researcher must therefore be guided by reasonable assumptions, sometimes called regularity conditions, to arrive at conclusions which will closely approximate facts, usually referred to as principles, when facts could not be conclusively established.

The pursuit of facts for making generalizations is one of the major reasons why research in the social sciences has become so fascinating. There is arguably no theory which has a monopoly over the explanation of human conduct. This encourages relentless inquiry in the quest of a guiding principle. Research ultimately becomes important for a number of reasons including the following: profit maximization; attaining good health; improving technology; expanding knowledge; and making policy. A firm, for example, would be interested in knowing how to exploit human preferences or taste to maximize profit. It would also be important to know whether stem cell research might help to cure Alzheimer's disease, or whether the use of more fuel efficient cars could necessarily contribute to the reduction of global warming.

The interest of firms in human consumption behavior could easily interact with other prevailing conditions—the state of unemployment, the prices of competitive goods, the cost of production, or the policies of other firms in the industry. This makes it more plausible to deal with multivariate models than univariate ones. The profit maximizing firm would therefore be well served by investing more in the understanding of precedents, theories of profit maximization or loss minimization, and other interactive variables.

Apart from the much more vocational essence of research, there are times when research takes on a purely academic dimension—writing a research paper or a dissertation because of an academic requirement. These are invariably far from worthless exercises. The general underlying principle is normally to revisit a past or prevailing controversy in order to verify or challenge a prior finding, or come up with a pioneering idea and result. Evidently this does not destabilize the motive for research, but rather, it makes the motive of research more robust in the search of what could be perceived of as a more credible or factual response to a controversy, or a more innovative enquiry. Controversial topics abound in the social sciences. For example, does an increase in the minimum wage lead to unemployment or not; are couples making $40 thousand a year or less likely to get an early divorce; what factors would cause males to earn more than females; are black neighborhoods crime infested or not; is the demand for marijuana price elastic or not; is poverty the result of laziness or lack of opportunities; is religion an obstruction to scientific progress or not? Though these issues expose researchers to the realities of life, and help them to make independent discoveries as critical thinking academic exercises; they also have policy ramifications. Research into these issues is generally undertaken with the motive of making persuasive arguments to influence policy making.

Political parties and policy makers still have stark differences over economic policies and economic well being. These differences are far from novel. Some of the most interesting ones date back to the seventeenth and eighteenth centuries, and they largely concern the role of government. For example, in the eighteenth century French physiocrats made the argument that economic activities should obey the natural laws of nature—meaning that the role of government in regulating economic activity should be minimal. This concept was later popularized by Adam Smith in his celebrated work, *The Wealth of Nations* (1776).

Indeed the so called "free market" theory was popular for quite some time, until changing circumstances challenged its validity. One of the major events which challenged its pristine form was the American Great Depression of the 1930s. The pure market system turned out to be flawed and fallible as unemployment soared and output plummeted in an environment of financial chaos. Today, political scientists, and economists debate over the extent of government intervention. For example, should the government regulate trade; is an increase in the money supply inflationary; should tax cuts be made permanent; can government policies stabilize or destabilize an economy; should a government encourage transfer payments; is there a trade off between equity and growth; is the environment being irreparably assaulted? These are just some of the many controversial issues facing contemporary governments which also attract the attention of researchers.

The potential for making profit may be plentiful, just as the controversies that excite research. The serious researcher is always confronted with many challenges which demand prudent thought and method. It is not uncommon for researchers to try to popularize their opinions or preconceived notions of a controversy. When notions of biases are injected into the methodology of a research, the outcomes may become misleading, fallacious, or spurious. This makes it necessary for the sources of information, and the logic underlying the premise to be transparent so that others could determine the basis of a conclusion. The goal of research is not to affirm an opinion, although an unbiased procedure could happily converge with an opinion.

In the real world the injection of ego into the research process or the inability to separate opinion from objective research could be a crisis phenomenon; especially for supervised researchers with egomaniacal supervisors. Some early writers do not necessarily like their theories to be challenged, and as such, they would try to eternalize their findings. This normally sets a stage for confrontation and agony in the research process. Some others would have very little appetite for deviation from their own way of thinking. This results in loss of independence and threatens the potential to enjoy a reasonable measure of critical thinking. The results of these problems are telling—frustration and pain. Supervised researchers will be well advised to know the mannerisms of their supervisors if they have an option of choosing their supervisors.

It is not uncommon for major disagreements to arise over a research position which challenges popular theories. When there is phobia of challenging "sacrosanct theories", data, model, and conclusions have to be forged to conform to normal sentiments and findings. The forgery is normally predicated on what is known as "data mining".

Researchers who are obsessed with preconceived notions tend to search for variables and data that are well correlated to a perceived conclusion. The fundamental premise of the research—the hypothesis, is deliberately developed around such a correlation. The elements of surprise and randomness are generally sacrificed. This problem is typical of structural models in which a dependent variable is set up to have a functional relationship with other variable(s). The basic idea is to explain a phenomenon which is related to why something is happening and/or what might be the effect of the explanatory variable(s)—the variables on the right hand side of an equation, on the dependent variable—the variable that is to be explained on the left hand side. For example, researchers might want to know why an interest rate would go up or down.

There could be other issues of interest. Why would consumers spend more or less? Why would investors be attracted to a particular country? Why would people save more or less? What is the effect of an increase in the money supply on interest rate? What is the effect of more education on wages? Why is the level of carbon monoxide increasing? What is the effect of an increase on the level of carbon monoxide in atmospheric pollution? What are the economic effects on a domestic economy of skilled or unskilled international migration? These questions manifest cause-effect analysis which is normally a precondition for undertaking research.

On the other side of the spectrum is forecasting, which involves the probability of an event occurring, and making decisions based on chance occurrences which are projected to be reasonably accurate and based on data and/or models. Speculators would like to know for example, what would be the dollar-yen exchange rate four or six months from today in New York and London so that they could make profit through arbitrage. Speculators thrive on calculated risks which are dependent on their ability to make good projections or forecasts. The sellers of BMWs would like to know the prospects of selling more BMWs next year or two years from today so that they could plan on how to make hiring and inventory decisions. The managers will be well served to make educated projections. If you were an investor in a particular company you would also want to know the growth potential of that company. You may be interested in the projected earnings of the company as much as the liabilities of the company, if not its net worth. You will therefore need a reasonable understanding of the future growth of that company.

It is probably apparent by now that normal research would be driven by an underlying interest or motive that is attractive to the researcher. It would be extremely problematic to embark on a research project if the topic is jejune, and if the researcher feels no compelling attachment to the inquiry. This is so because research entails a high degree of commitment to achieving an end result through what could be a very time consuming and painful process. A lack of commitment would only result in frustration and/or abandonment of a research project.

Starting the research process requires knowledge of a topic of interest. This is not an easy task for a beginner who has just been asked to do a research paper or who is thinking about one for the very first time. Even much more advanced researchers may have difficulty selecting a topic for research. This is normal for a variety of reasons. Invariably most topics have already been visited or revisited. It is like beating a dead horse because the act of undertaking research is not a recent phenomenon. On other occasions a topic might not come to mind. On such occasions researchers are therefore at a loss as they ponder over what exactly they should write on. They literally freeze.

There are, however, ways of dealing with the problems of inertia. First, it is usually advisable to think of a topic. It would be amazing to know how this first step leads into myriads of delightful unintended consequences. It is not uncommon for researchers to deal with issues that they never imagined as they get deeper into the research process. Topics can take simple forms; for example, the sale of Toyotas in the US and Japan; seasonal employment in the US and company output; the availability of credit and consumption of a durable good; unemployment and credit availability; tax credit and purchases; credit and liability index; the effect of variable cost on output; and the effect of technological improvement on cost and output.

The selection of a topic is only the beginning of an unsettling process. The researcher must then decide how to deal with the topic or what should be in the thesis that would drive the entire research process. This is not necessarily an easy matter. One way of confronting the task is to take a look at what others have done or said regarding the topic of interest. Doing so requires substantial reading and research on the topic. Fortunately the Internet can be exploited in very constructive ways. A search for "credit" on the Internet, for example, could produce thousands of results. The researcher who had originally started with no clear clue as to what he wanted to do is suddenly overwhelmed by a host of information from which he has to pick and choose.

By methodically going through the information now at hand the researcher gets to see what others have said about the topic, and might immediately develop a critical opinion about what he is reading. The adventure now takes the form of comparing and contrasting information and assessing the probabilities of which argument is cogent or implausible. Every piece of information becomes critical. Books on the topics now become relevant. Refereed journal articles become golden, news paper articles are now pursued avidly and periodicals are thrown into the mix. Information becomes an unfathomable abyss. Footnotes, references or bibliography now complicate the amount of information at the disposal of the researcher for which he now has to narrow his focus.

One of the most intricate questions then becomes who is correct in the face of contending findings. Alternatively, are there issues that have been oversighted and have not been considered? How could such issues change the dynamics or results of the prior arguments and shape subsequent studies? The logical extension of the questions quickly becomes how events are to be explained and modeled. In quick succession, the decision on a topic leads to acquiring information which arouses curiosity that is ultimately couched in the form of a thesis and a model. Yet greater problems lie ahead—collecting appropriate and credible data, and estimating and testing the plausibility of the findings.

Sampling

It is important to recall that the whole idea of undertaking a research revolves around obtaining a result that would meaningfully help to evaluate a theory, arrive at a principle, corroborate a fact, or generate profit. It is therefore vital to have a sample that would credibly lead to convincing results. It is not uncommon for the availability of data to have a significant effect on the determination of a sample size. This makes the exploration of data availability an equally serious matter as developing a hypothesis. It would be meaningless to have a very nice and erudite hypothesis for which there is no data—simply put, the hypothesis could not be evaluated. Presenting a topic for a research, without exploring the possibilities of getting the required data, may result in the premature withdrawal from a topic. It is important to note that exploring the possibilities of data availability is not synonymous with data mining. Premature withdrawal of a topic might give the appearance of inadequate preparation or indecisiveness. This might also be a first cause of frustration with the research process.

Since the object of undertaking the research is to have worthwhile results that would positively respond to the research motive, it is essential to investigate a large number of events or occurrences. This idea is closely associated with what is known as the *Law of Averages*. To understand the *Law of Averages* two concepts are key—population and sample.

Population refers to the complete set of objects of interest. In theory it is the collection of all outcomes, responses, measurements or counts that are of interest to the researcher. It is by definition unobtainable because generally researchers are not able to access all the objects of interest. For example, suppose a researcher is interested in knowing the impact of computer ownership on the purchases of magazines, or knowing the effects of debit cards on the purchases of digital video discs (DVDs). It is evident that the researcher would never be able to know all the owners of computers, as well as all those who own computers and are also making magazine purchases. He would not also be able to obtain data on all the holders of debit cards who are purchasing DVDs. He is therefore confronted with a dilemma of how best to obtain information that would approximate the population which he is trying to get.

The first inclination might be a problematic one—using counts of a population that are readily available without including those which are not readily available. This type of sampling is generally considered a sample of convenience that is likely to produce unreliable results because of the exclusion of other relevant parts of the population. A comparatively deeper thought of a sampling method would provide the researcher alternative methods of sampling. Apart from the random, these methods could be classified as systematic, clustered, or stratified. These alternative options must be used with some amount of precaution as they typically exhibit flaws of their own; especially lack of variation if the sample is arranged and the variables are categorical.

A systematic sample is one for which a sub/sample is selected from a grand sample (population) by selecting the *k*th subject/observation from the grand sample. To determine the sub/sample size the researcher must determine the *k*th subject/observation to be included in his sub/sample. The grand-sample to *k*th-observation ratio ultimately determines the sample size. For example, a grand sample size of 600 from which every 20th observation is to be included will yield a sub-sample of 600/20 or 30. Alternatively, a sub-sample to grand-sample ratio of 1/6 (assuming a sub/sample size of 100 is desired), would indicate that the starting point must be from the sixth observation and systematically in that sequence going forward. Subjectivity bias is largely contingent on the type of variable investigated and pre-sampling considerations or foreknowledge of the grand sample. A cluster sample is similar to a systematic sample in the sense that it is also a sub-sample.

A cluster sample is a sample derived from clusters or groups. A population is divided into groups/clusters. This form of sampling is normally deemed to be desirable when a geographical population is scattered and it becomes impractical to be able to reach individuals of a population. For example the population of a town could be divided into households which consist of individuals. From the households, a sample could be drawn to reflect individual characteristics. This is generally known as the "random sampling of clusters."

The collection of data based on a stratified sample involves the division of the sample into strata because of a shared characteristic, which might be the result of socio-economic or income differentials. In this case each segment of a population is represented. The idea of inclusion makes stratified samples more attractive than simple random samples when status, race, age, gender, and religious and/or political ideologies are involved.

By making a decision to approximate the population, the researcher is actively pursuing the idea of collecting information that would best be representative of the population which he is otherwise unable to get. In short, he is looking at the prospect of collecting a reasonable sample that would replace the population or act as a surrogate of the population without any significant difference. This requires a large sample size which would be indicative of a normal distribution. A simple sample or random sample is one in which every member of the population has an equal chance of being selected.

There are good statistical or econometric reasons for the sample size to be large. Apart from targeting the elusive population, there has to be an element of randomness so that the sample is not biased. For example, if a researcher wants to know whether an increase in advertising increases the sale of Polo Jeans, he is likely to get a much more accurate result if he chooses a sample that includes males and females, young and old, rich and poor and slim and obese. Choosing a sample of a collection of slim teenagers who are fond of wearing Polo Jeans would yield a biased and deceptive result. Drawing conclusions from such a sample and making policies based on such a sample would be dangerously misleading and might detrimentally increase the cost of marketing and reduce profits.

The option to use a sample is based on a probability distribution which is generally tied to a *Law of Averages*. The rationale behind the *Law of Averages* is that the average of independent observations of random variables with the same probability distribution is increasingly likely to be closest to the expected value of the random variables as the number of observations (samples) increases. Two issues should be immediately cleared up.

By relating samples to probability two important concepts have been introduced: (i) the average of independent observations of random variables; and (ii) a normal distribution. A variable is defined as random when its value is randomly chosen from a population or when its value is subject to random variation. In actual fact the word "variable" connotes randomness in research, and random may be otherwise seen as redundant. The average, which is also known as the mean, is a measure of location. The average could take the form of an arithmetic mean, a weighted mean, or a geometric mean. It is the central value around which the values of a data would cluster. The researcher would therefore like his observations to be as close to the value of the expected mean as possible.

The average is therefore a measure of central tendency and a powerful piece of information to determine how close or far away other values are situated from it. Other measures of central tendency are the median (the middle data entry when the data is well ordered) and the mode (the entry with the most frequency). Knowledge of the average facilitates three important measures of variation: (i) mean absolute deviation; (ii) variance; and (iii) standard deviation.

Knowledge of the average enables the development of a Central Limit Theorem, which holds that averaging almost always leads to a bell-shaped distribution for which the majority of the values of the data would be clustered around the mean while the minority would taper off away from the mean with the tails of the bell-shaped curve asymptotically reaching zero. This is a powerful theory which allows for standardization around a mean.

Just what is considered a large enough sample to fit the bell-shaped paradigm? Ideally, the rule of thumb is that the researcher is expected to have at least thirty observations. Researchers have more often than not exceeded this benchmark considerably, at times by more than three hundred percent or more. This is not entirely surprising because they have tried to approximate the population of their various interests to the best of their abilities. This approach is consistent with the *Law of Averages*. Assuming normality, the distribution of a random variable with infinite values has a probability density function for which the parameters to be estimated, the mean and variance, are zero and one respectively.

The assumption of normality means that 68% of a data which is hypothetically believed to have a normal distribution would fall within one standard deviation of the mean; 95% within two standard deviations and 99.7% within three standard deviations. The Chebychev's Theorem scores the proportion as 75% for two standard deviations, and 88.9% for three standard deviations. The claim of normality and knowledge of standard deviation are crucial for hypothesis testing. The z-value is used as a test statistic to know whether the claim of a hypothesized value could be rejected or not (i.e.) a failure to reject, which does not mean acceptance. Two errors are possible when rejecting the null or failing to reject the null—rejecting the null when it is true (type I error), and failing to reject the null when it is false (type II error). For samples which are smaller than thirty observations, the t distribution and statistic are used.

Data

To a very large extent sample size is largely contingent on data availability. Data is information which comes from observations, counts, and responses. Data may be extraordinarily plentiful or scarce. They should however be received with great precaution. The caution is essential to maintain the integrity of the research motive. Bad data generates bad results and defeats the purpose of the research endeavor. The researcher is consequently obligated to check the source and quality of the data before proceeding with his analysis.

Data could be numerical (in the form of real numbers—1, 2, 3,-1,-2...) or categorical (in the form of characteristics—male, female, black, white, Hispanic...). Depending on the type of analysis to be made, categorical variables could be ascribed numerical values. For example, 1 for black and 0 for white. When such a transformation is made, the variable is said to be a dummy. Hence the phrase "dummy variables". Variables are measurable characteristics which take varying values. For example, a wage is a variable if it takes values of $200, $300, or even $1000 a week over time. The opposite of a variable is a constant. A constant does not change, and therefore the change of a constant is always zero.

To avoid falling into the *dummy variable trap* in regression analysis, it is required that the number of dummies selected be one less than the number of categorical variables. A researcher who is caught by this trap would have results which show perfect multicolinearity—a situation in which two or more explanatory/independent variables in a regression model are highly correlated so that it becomes difficult or impractical to separate or isolate the individual effects on the dependent variable (the variable to be explained).

Data may also be analyzed from three perspectives: (i) time series; (ii) cross-section; and (iii) pooled. Time series data show a chronological sequence of observations on a particular variable. Two concepts are key—time progression and a particular variable. Time series data may be compiled daily, monthly, quarterly or annually, and they are very useful for forecasting, but they pose a problem of nonstationarity which could be dealt with by contemporary statistical software. For example, Eviews is well constructed to deal with such problems.

One of the most challenging problems of time series data is that of nonstationarity. Stationarity requires that the mean and variance of a random/stochastic process to be constant, and that the value of the covariance is dependent on the lag value between two time periods and not the time at which the covariance is computed. The problem of nonstationarity stems from the very nature of time series data which exhibits trends, cycles, seasonal variations, and irregular fluctuations.

Cross-section data are data on one or more variables collected at the same point in time. As such, they are data on many units, such as individuals, households, firms, governments or countries at the same time. They are otherwise known as parallel data. A familiar problem with cross-section data is heterogeneity. As a factual matter, some nations or firms are big, and others small; some are wealthier, and others, poorer; some nations are densely populated and others are relatively sparsely populated. To do regression analysis with meaningful policy implications, these differences have to be adjusted for. For example, it may be wise to use per capita gross domestic product (GDP), or per capita consumption rather than the GDP of a nation or total national consumption, when various countries are part of the analysis. Scaling the data down to per unit measure may also be wise when firms of various sizes and income are involved in the analysis.

Pooled data are data which combine the elements of time series and cross-section data. A special type of pooled data is the longitudinal or micropanel data, which is also known as panel data. In a panel data the same cross-sectional unit is surveyed over time. Table. 1 summarizes the categories of data.

Table: 1
Data Types

Time Series		**Cross-Section /Pooled**		**Panel**		
Year	NYSE (Avg. Daily Trade Volume $)	Minimum wage (2004/5)		Mortgage Backed securities Issuances ($ Billions)		
1999	809M	Alaska	$7.15	Fannie Mae	1999	270
2000	1042M	Washington	$7.16		2000	179
2001	1240M	Oregon	$7.05		2001	483
2002	1441M	Georgia	$5.15	Freddie Mac	1999	216
2003	1398M	New York	$5.15		2000	139
2004	1442M	Texas	$5.15		2001	254

Estimation

To acquire good results, the researcher must be able to identify the theory or theories he is interested in before estimating his data. This is so, because estimation must be guided by a model specification. Apart from correlation, Granger-Causality, and Vector Auto-regressive analyses, estimation would require some kind of structural model with a dependent variable and independent variable(s). This structural form is normally estimated by regression analysis—regressing the dependent variable on the independent variable(s).

The classical regression model makes specific assumptions: (i) that the mean value of the error in a model specification is zero and has a normal distribution; (ii) there is no serial correlation (i.e.) observations of the error term in one period do not show up in another time period or affect the error term in another period (the errors are uncorrelated with each other); (iii) all explanatory variables are uncorrelated with the error term; (iv) the error term must have a constant variance (i.e.) the variance of the distribution of the error term for each observation must be the same (homoskedastic); and (v) no explanatory variable should be a perfect linear function of another. A violation of this assumption causes multicolinearity. For example, if a researcher is interested in explaining individual consumption, his model would be misspecified if it is expressed in terms of income, wealth, savings, preferences/taste, and prices. Wealth is correlated with income and savings. To be parsimonious and avoid multicolinearity, consumption could be explained in terms of wealth, preferences, and prices. Income, wealth, and savings are all positively and strongly correlated to one another, and wealth is a good proxy of the others.

Regression analysis is a statistical technique that attempts to explain the relationship between a dependent variable on the right hand side (RHS) and the independent or exogenous variable(s) on the left hand side (LHS). Although it is tempting to see the RHS variable and the LHS variable(s) in terms of a cause-effect relationship, regression does not necessarily imply causality. It is merely a way of finding out the expected value of the dependent, given the independent variable(s) when the population of the independent variable(s) is not exactly known—a conditional probability expressed as a population regression function (PRF). The dependent variable is explained based on a unit change of an independent variable when the others are held constant. This relationship is normally defined by a slope coefficient. The slope or rate of change in Economics is a very useful concept which is otherwise understood in terms of elasticity or marginalism.

Specification is usually a reflection of a theory. Under exceptional circumstances, a *prima facie* understanding of the data should help with model specification. For example, the distribution of data points of a variable which resemble a parabola would normally indicate that a quadratic specification may be necessary for that variable. Variables which have an exponent of one are considered linear. When they are raised to an exponent greater than one they are considered nonlinear.

Regression models may be specified in various forms, and may take slightly different connotations when the objectives and specifications are different. For example, although causal relationships are not typically implied in cross-sectional analysis, a forecasting model with two or more variables may be defined as a *causal forecasting model.* On the other hand, a model in which a variable is regressed on its past values for the purpose of forecasting is considered univariate.

Intercept terms may precede the combination of slope coefficients in model specifications, and error terms may be included at the end of specifications to account for those variables which have been left out or oversighted. Eviews makes provision for omitted variables test, the Hausman test and other specification tests. The typical regression model could be broken up into two parts—the deterministic component, which excludes the error term, and could best be described in terms of the expected value of the dependent variable given the independent variable(s), and the stochastic/random segment, which is captured by the error term.

Cross-sectional models could be bivariate (a-two variable model—one dependent and one independent), multivariate (more-than-two-variable regression model), or simultaneous (a system of equations). Estimation of regression models might require the transformation of the raw data to meet the objective(s) of the researcher. Data could be compiled into averages of three or more years. It is important to note, however, that averages of shorter periods provide for persistence and make it feasible for one variable to be a better predictor of the other.

Simultaneous models are notorious for endogeneity problems when used for cross-sectional analysis, and serial correlation, when used for time series analysis. Endogeneity problems arise when an independent variable in an equation of a system of equations is also a dependent variable in another equation of the system. Estimation of such models without rectification, leads to biased results or spurious/nonsense regression. Luckily Eviews and other statistical software have been designed to deal with such problems easily. The classic solution is normally the use of an instrumental variable—a variable which is correlated with the independent variables but not the errors. A prominent estimator to deal with this type of problem is the 2-stage Least Squares (2sls), alternatively known as an instrumental variable (IV) estimator. Although lagged variables are easy instruments, they may not be altogether suitable. It is always a good idea to experiment with others which make theoretical sense.

The successful use of 2sls requires the observance of preconditions for identification. Identification is essential for numerical estimates to be obtained from structural models. As such the model must not be overidentified or underidentified. It must meet the order and rank conditions: (i) the number of predetermined or independent variables excluded from an equation must not be less than the number of endogenous or dependent variables in that equation less one; and (ii) in a model with the same amount of dependent variables as there are equations, for example 3 and 3, an equation is identified if one nonzero determinant of the order (3-1)(3-1) can be constructed from the coefficients of the variables excluded from that particular equation, but included in the other equations of the model. The rank condition could be intimidating and makes for good academic exercise. Good estimating software however, barely requires users to specify their instruments. Knowledge of the order and rank condition is nevertheless helpful to input information into the computer.

As part of the specification process, the researcher must then decide whether he wants to run his regression as a double log model (constant elasticity model), which gives a constant slope coefficient; a log-lin model, in which the slope coefficient measures the constant change in the dependent variable for a given change in the independent variable or its lin-log counterpart.

Estimation without hypothesis testing is rarely complete. It is then incumbent on the researcher to test his coefficients or models appropriately. Most statistical packages are well suited to meet this challenge. For example, Eviews provides opportunities for a Wald Test, heteroskedasticity test, serial correlation test, Lagrange Multiplier test, Cointegration test, or even joint coefficient tests. The analysis of variance which is immediately reported also provides an intuitive indication of how well the model has performed. It is always a good idea to check whether the t-statistic is greater than 2 for significant coefficients at the 95% level of confidence.

Exercises on Why Research

1. Select a financial or economic topic of interest and explain why you find that topic interesting.

2. Briefly describe what others have said about a topic. What do you find puzzling or interesting about what others have said? If some areas of the topic have not been fully explained or discussed explain what has been left out or given inadequate attention.

3. How would you develop a thesis statement around this topic based on your exposure to it? How important is your topic to national policy or institutional and/or private income?

4. What type of data do you think you will need to explore the relevant areas of the topic you have chosen? Why? What problems do you foresee with data availability or possible inquiry?

5. Identify two or more recent controversies over a Finance or Economics topic. How could research help you to take a position on the topic? How would you decide on the amount of information required to convince you about your results? What do you expect to find from your research? How would you estimate your data?

CHAPTER 2

DATA SOURCES

Apart from sample size and estimating strategy, good empirical results depend on the sources from which data are obtained. The researcher needs to identify the sources of information to ensure the transparency of method and validity of the research results. Precautionary guidelines are therefore warranted.

First, the researcher must ensure that the institution or avenue from which data is collected is reputable and credible. Second, he must verify whether or not information is filtered and distorted, or whether the prospects of tampering with information are real. Third, it is important to understand the characterization of the variables and the units in which they are measured. Fourth, it may be pertinent to know how information is collected, and whether or not the institution/avenue providing the data is stringently supervised and regulated. Some researchers would make use of sources that are generally renowned and have been the conduit of reputable findings and publication in the past. These sources are generally cited in publications. Credible sources are many, but most fall beyond the scope of this work, and they will not be discussed here.

The New York Stock Exchange (NYSE)[1]

The NYSE was founded in 1792, and is the largest equities market place in the world. The stocks of the largest and best known corporations in America and the rest of the world are traded in the NYSE also known as the "Big Board". It is an unincorporated association governed by a board of directors headed by a chairman. The board is composed of individuals representing the public and the exchange membership. To meet investor security the NYSE has corporate governance rules which regulate conflict of interests and disclosures to protect investors through fair trading and to ensure efficiency.

The exchange does not buy or sell stock, and as such does not gain or lose on any given trading day. It barely provides a medium where people and institutions buy and sell stocks on a daily basis through agents and brokers. The prices of these stocks are not set by the NYSE, but are determined by auction through a traditional outcry.

In a typical free market environment, buyers compete for the lowest prices as sellers compete to sell at the highest prices. This free market environment has evolved from the gloomy days of the 1860s and 1920s when stock values were inflated (watered stock), and "bear-raids" manipulated/rigged the market, to the much more regulated and transparent contemporary system, *albeit* an imperfect one.

Indeed the unfettered follies of the old way of doing things climaxed in the 1930s with the Great Depression. The Securities and Exchange Commission (SEC) was established in 1934 with an important objective of preventing, the manipulation or rigging of the market, which defrauded investors and threatened the stability of the market and the world economy in the 1930s.

Engel and Hecht (1994) observe that there "is probably no business in the world that operates under more stringent regulation or with a stricter self-imposed code of ethics than the modern-day New York Stock Exchange". [2] Price and volume movements of all stocks traded in the exchange are kept under computerized stock-watching surveillance to flag any unusual movements in a stock, to be followed by an investigation. The stringent rules for membership and method of operation make the NYSE an organized market.

The data collected by the NYSE, as at this writing, could be classified under seven broad headings: (i) reported share volume records; (ii) monthly turnover rates; (iii) NYSE statistics archive; (iv) program trading statistics; (v) monthly block volume/largest block transactions; (vi) round lots; and non US data.

The *reported share volume records* shows recorded trading volume by year, quarter, month, week, day and first hour. *Monthly turnover rates* lists annualized turnover for a given month. This is calculated by multiplying the average daily volume for the month by the number of trading days in the current year and dividing the product by the total shares outstanding at the end of the month.[3] *The NYSE statistics archive* provides historical information on trading activity for free. *Program trading statistics* gives a range of portfolio trading strategies dealing with the purchase or sale of a basket of at least fifteen stocks with a total value of $1million or more. *Monthly block volume transactions* lists the largest block volume trades for past twelve months and the ten largest block transactions for the year. Block trades are considered to be trades equal to or greater than 10,000 shares. *Round lots* give the average daily volume of round lots (shares and warrants) for NYSE members. *Non US data* provides statistics on annual volume and value of trading, and trading history for non US firms.

Data on stock trading may be useful to do both forecasting and cross-sectional analysis in the following areas: investment, consumer confidence, the performance of the US economy, reaction to interest rate and/or price changes whether they are real, imagined or expected.

The Federal Reserve (Fed)[4]

The Federal Reserve was established as a central bank system of the US by a Congressional Act of 1913. The idea of a nationally chartered bank that would exercise control over the money supply in America was passionately advocated for by Alexander Hamilton. The Bank of Pennsylvania which was originally established in 1781 as a state bank, was asked to function as a central bank in 1791 for twenty years. Its life thereafter was contingent on congressional approval. Between 1791 and 1913, the history of the US central bank is a chequered record of intermittent charter renewal.

There were specific reasons for the establishment of a central bank system in the US. Run on the banks, premature recall of loans, financial insecurity, loss of confidence in the banking system, less prudent investment, and lack of supervision and regulation which culminated in financial crises, confirmed the urgent need for a central bank. One of the most remarkable crises was the Knickerbocker Trust disaster of 1907 in New York.

Unlike other central banks of the world, the Fed is independently owned by member banks and is supposed to be insulated from the influence of partisan politics. It was created by an Act of Congress, and Congress retains the right to abolish it, yet, it is supposed to function without political pressures to make monetary policies that would not be driven by political decisions or influences. Some of the policy tools at the disposal of the Fed include: (i) the selling and buying of securities; (ii) increasing or decreasing the discount rate (the rate which the Fed charges depository institutions for borrowing from the Fed); and (iii) increasing or decreasing the reserve requirement (the proportion of deposits which depository institutions must hold as vault cash or on deposit with the Fed). Increasing the money supply is a deliberate attempt to encourage expansion of credit to stimulate economic growth. It is not synonymous with printing money. Increasing the cost of borrowing money is normally a defensive posture to check money growth or inflation.

As a political and economic compromise the Fed is a decentralized system of twelve district banks and twenty-five branches. The decentralization makes the services of the central bank available to diverse regions and interests in a country that is almost the size of the North American continent and which had been troubled by polarizing agrarian (southern) and industrial (northern) interests.

The Federal Reserve maintains an eclectic collection of financial data on daily, weekly, monthly, quarterly, or annual indicators, some of which involve commercial paper, loan charge-offs, medium term notes, interest rates, and monetary base. Fed data could broadly be aggregated under the following general headings: (i) principal economic indicators; (ii) bank asset quality; (iii) bank structure data; (iv) business finance; (v) exchange rates and international data;

(vi) household finance; (vii) industrial activity; (viii) interest rates; (ix) bank assets and liabilities; (x) flow of funds accounts; and (xi) money stock and reserve balances.

Data are provided for seasonally adjusted/deseasonalized and unadjusted consumer credit, with a breakdown of the providers of credits (financial institutions or intermediaries, as well as the cost of borrowing (interest rates), pools of securitized assets, and the type of credit—revolving and non-revolving.

Charge-offs and delinquency rates on loans and leases at commercial banks are compiled from the quarterly Federal Financial Institutions Examinations Council (FFIEC) consolidated reports of condition and income. Delinquency and charge-off rates are recorded for transactions involving real estates and mortgages, in seasonally and non-seasonally adjusted formats for large banks (with consolidated assets of $300 million or more), and smaller depository institutions.

Data on daily, weekly, and monthly commercial paper rates, unsecured short-term (less than one year) debt obligations, issued by banks, corporations, and other borrowers to investors are accounted for. The data on commercial paper is supplied by The Depository Trust Company (DTC), which is a national clearinghouse for the settlement of securities trades and a custodian for securities. Companies occasionally use commercial paper to raise money for current transactions as an alternative to costlier bank loans. Commercial paper rates are indexed. The Fed uses DTC's data for certain trades to estimate a relation between interest rates on the traded securities and their maturities.

The business finance section also provides data on the rates of interest on the loans provided by finance companies for businesses, real estates, and consumers. Information collected by The Survey of Small Business Finances (businesses with fewer than 500 employees) contain information about owner characteristic, firm size, income, financial services, and the balance sheet of small businesses.

Firms conducting international operations would normally benefit from knowledge of international data on exchange rates, credit availability, and levels of corruption associated with doing international business. Although the Fed does not provide data on levels of international corruption, it provides substantial information on foreign exchange rates. A fuller understanding of the gyrations of exchange rates is pretty difficult, but over the years some speculators have done fairly well with guessing or forecasting the gyrations of exchange rates. The Fed reports the rate of foreign currencies per dollar on a daily basis, in addition to the maintenance of a historical archive of exchange rates. Information on dollar indexes, and geometric weighted averages of the dollar exchange rate (with due consideration to international trade) are also provided.

The Home Mortgage Disclosure Act (1975) is implemented by the Federal Reserve Board. This Act requires lending institutions to report public loan data. A summary of mortgage and home improvement lending data prepared yearly by individual lenders is made available by FFIEC. Institutions are provided a guide as to how they can report disclosures and step-by-step data. Home purchase loans (including refinancing) as well as home improvement loans are reported.

The Fed also releases data on industrial production and capacity utilization, which is a monthly index of industrial production and related capacity indexes and capacity utilization. The compilation covers manufacturing, mining and electric and gas utilities. The industrial detail of the measures indicates structural changes in the economy.

The production index measures real output as a percentage of a base year real output.[5] The capacity index is an estimate of sustainable potential output which is also expressed as a percentage of actual output using a base year. The production indexes are computed as Fisher indexes since 1972. Weights are based on annual estimates of value added. The rate of capacity utilization is a seasonally adjusted output index expressed as a percentage of the related capacity index.

Information on excess reserves and the monetary base is crucial to analyzing expansionary and contractionary monetary policies, as much as an increase or decrease in interest rate. Record of the aggregate reserves of depository institutions and the monetary base could also be obtained from the Fed. On a weekly basis, the Fed publishes data on aggregate reserves of depository institutions. These include: (i) required reserves; (ii) total reserves; (iii) excess reserves; (iii) nonborrowed reserves; and (iv) borrowings by depository institutions from the Federal Reserve's discount window. Interest rates for selected US Treasury and private money and capital market instruments are published on a weekly basis. US real interest rate may be used as an instrumental variable to determine investment in foreign countries.

Bureau of Labor Statistics (BLS)[6]

The BLS is an agency of the Department of Labor (DOL). The mission statement of the BLS indicates that it is the principal fact finding agency for the Federal government in the general field of labor economics and statistics. It is an independent national statistical agency that *collects, processes, analyzes, and disseminates essential statistical data to the American public, the US Congress, other Federal agencies, State and local governments, business and labor.*

The BLS data deals with relevant current economic and social issues, timelines which reflect changing economic conditions, and provides accurate and consistently high statistical quality reflecting impartiality in subject matter and presentation.

The DOL came into being on March 4, 1913 under President William Howard Taft. The creation of the department was the a result of a relentless campaign by organized labor, as much as the product of the progressive movement in the 1900s for better working conditions, conservation of natural resources, and opportunities for profitable employment.

The changing economic conditions, since its inception, have expanded its statutory responsibilities and mission. However, the collection of statistical data and dissemination of economic and statistical information constitute an integral component of the department's mission.

During the interregnum of the World Wars the department was embroiled in turbulence involving labor movements and communists, culminating in a *Red Scare hysteria*—a manifestation of xenophobia, labor strikes, race riots, expulsion of elected officials, and summary deportations of aliens, all of which, more often than not, bordered on a phobia of the intrusion of the ideals of *Bolsheviks*, *reds*, or communist. In the face of turmoil and adversity, the DOL has shown remarkable resilience.

The BLS, which was one of the four bureaus associated with the birth of the DOL, was created in 1884 to collect social and economic statistics and report on matters affecting working people.[7] In the late 1970s and early 1980s strong attempts were made to strengthen the quality and credibility of labor statistics. This was, and is still important for providing accurate information, developing plans and programs and evaluating plans and programs. Data collected is also important for the allocation of public funds and indexation of wages to adjust for the impact of inflation.

Major accomplishments of the BLS during the Carter Administration included a thorough review of labor force statistics by a presidential commission, a comprehensive revision of the Consumer Price Index (CPI—the index used to measure inflation), and an expansion and improvement of other economic measures produced by the BLS. For example, the bureau published two consumer price indexes in 1978—an updated version of the CPI for urban wage earners and clerical workers, and a new CPI for urban consumers.

In 1979, a nine-member National Commission on Employment and Unemployment Statistics found the labor force statistics to be sound. Improvements have been made on the industrial price program, employment cost index, the collection of occupational safety and health statistics, and an international price program.[8]

The CPI is one of the most leading indicators of inflation or periodic price changes. It is an index of typical urban consumption involving a range of goods that is published on a monthly basis by the BLS. The CPI is generally based on the prices of food, clothing, shelter, transportation fares, charges for doctors' and dentists' services, drugs, and other goods and services that consumers buy for day-to-day living.

Prices are collected in 87 urban areas across the US from about 50,000 housing units and approximately 23,000 retail establishments—department stores, supermarkets, hospitals, filling stations and other types of stores and service establishments. Taxes associated with purchases and uses of items are included in the index. Price changes for the various items in each location are averaged together with weights which represent the size in the spending of the relevant population group. Local data are then combined to obtain a US city average.[9]

The CPI is normally reported in deseasonalized and non-adjusted forms. Itemized reports provide an opportunity to make comparative assessments as to what items are more or less affected by price changes. It should be recalled that all indices have bases. More contemporaneously, the CPI for urban consumers uses 1982-84, while that of urban wage earners and clerical workers uses 1999. All bases use 100 as a benchmark.

Data on unemployment, employment, and discouraged workers are also provided by the BLS with specific definitional clarifications. Employment is positively and strongly correlated with income and consumption. A firm wishing to make projections about consumption of its goods would therefore wisely pay close attention to the level of employment and the economic temper of the times.

There is not generally a widespread agreement on how to measure employment, but analyses could be made against specific theoretical guidelines as prescribed by the BLS. A person is considered to be employed in the US if he has worked during a reference week and has been paid for that work; worked without pay at least for fifteen hours in a family business or farm; or is deemed to be temporarily absent from a job because of illness, vacation, labor-management disputes, or personal reasons.

People are generally classified as unemployed in the US, if they had no employment during the reference week although they were available to work at that time; if they made specific efforts to secure employment during the 4-week period ending with the reference week; or are laid off but expecting a recall.

The civilian labor force is the sum of employed and unemployed workers. Those not considered employed or unemployed are not counted in the labor force. Persons not in the labor force who want a job and are available for work, and have looked for a job for a year and are not currently looking because of loss of hope, either because they believe there is none or that they are not qualified, are considered "discouraged workers".

To deal with the seasonality associated with job availability, rather than the structural changes, the BLS adjusts its data (i.e.) deseasonalizes the data to expunge the effects of weather, production cycles, major holidays, and school sessions. It is estimated that seasonality has a 95 % impact on month to month changes in unemployment.

The BLS may be accessed for a variety of other reasons: (i) earnings by area occupation, and industry; (ii) state and local government unemployment rates; (iii) foreign labor statistics; (iv) US import price index; (v) demographic characteristics of the US labor force; and (vi) occupation injuries, illnesses and fatalities.

The Bureau of Economic Analysis (BEA)[10]

The BEA is an agency of the Department of Commerce (DOC). The mission statement of the bureau indicates that it is oriented toward the promotion of better understanding of the US economy by providing timely, relevant, and accurate economic accounts data in an objective and cost-effective manner. It sets as its vision the goal of being the world's most respected producer of economic accounts. Along with some other agencies, BEA is part of the DOC's Economics and Statistics Administration.

The DOC was founded in 1903, with an important objective of promoting American international trade, economic growth and technological advancement. The idea of creating a viable US commercial agency could probably be traced to 1897 when the Department of State created the Bureau of Foreign Commerce. The late 1890s was fortuitous for American trade. American factories were churning out more goods than the American public could consume. The production boom and growing importance of international trade, made it important for the US Department of Commerce to establish the Bureau of Foreign Commerce (BFC). One of the duties of the new agency was to provide commercial reports. The DOC which came into being in 1903 subsumed the BFC.

Since 1903 the DOC has developed to meet new challenges involving various facets of American commerce—aeronautics, maritime, communications, patents, and general transportation. The reorganizations and redefining of duties in the 1950s, particularly as they pertained to defense and commerce, led to the establishment of the Office of Business Economics (OBE). It was this office, OBE, that was ultimately renamed the BEA in 1972 when the Department's principal statistical agencies were being re-organized.

The "BEA produces economic accounts statistics that enable government and business decision-makers, researchers, and American public to follow and understand the performance of the Nation's economy."[11] To achieve its objectives the BEA collects source data, conducts research and analysis, develops and implements estimation methodologies, and releases statistics to the general public.

The BEA is one of the world's leading statistical agencies and its data are closely watched by policy makers, government officials, individuals, firms, and households. As such BEA data are instrumental in making monetary policy, tax and budget projections, and business investment plans. The BEA reports in 2005, that the GDP measure, which is featured in the National Income and Product Accounts (NIPAs), was recognized by the DOC as its greatest achievement of the 20th century. The measure is also recognized as one of the three most influential measures that affect US financial markets.

In addition to the NIPAs, which were originally developed after the American Great Depression of the late 1920s and early 1930s, the BEA has developed and extended its estimates to cover a diverse range of economic activities. Contemporary BEA data include important issues such as economic growth, regional economic development, interindustry relationships, and international economics, which are periodically tested for reliability.

BEA data could be classified under the following broad categories: (i) national; (ii) regional; (iii) industry; and (iv) international. National data deal with GDP and the central issues associated with the compilation or accuracy of GDP figures. Other features include: personal income and outlays, corporate profits, and fixed assets.

Regional data deal with state and local personal income, gross state product, and regional input-output multipliers (RIMS). RIMS is a method of analyzing the economic impacts of public- and private-sector projects and programs on affected/targeted regions. The method accounts for interindustry relationships within regions, since these relationships somehow determine how regional economies could potentially respond to project and program changes. Regional economic impact analysis is accounted for by regional input-output (I-O) multipliers. The method for estimating the I-O multipliers was developed in the 1970s based on the work of Garnick and Drake, but has since been improved. In 1997 the BEA published a handbook that provides more detail on the use of the multipliers and the data sources and methods for estimating them.[12] Industry data deal with annual industry accounts, GDP by industry, benchmark input-output accounts, and travel and tourism.

Economic indicators dealing with US international trade relations could be found in the international category. The statistics being disseminated include those dealing with the US balance of payments; US trade in goods and services with other countries; US international investment position; and direct investment. The BEA also provides interactive data, Papers and Working Papers, a glossary of terms, and frequently asked questions (FAQs) for further clarifications.

The Bureau of Census (BC)[13]

The BC is also an agency of the Department of Commerce. A cursory *prima facie* evidence of the word "census", might lead one to believe that the Department is only concerned with population count. In actual counting population is an original intention that has evolved to incorporate other salient indicators of US economic performance in keeping with a fact-finding tradition.

Since 1790 a census has been conducted in the US every ten years. Article 1, Section 2 of the United States Constitution required that representatives and direct taxes be apportioned according to the respective population of states. The continued expansion of America in the Nineteenth Century, at least in terms of population and consumption, made it necessary to focus on key indicators of production and consumption. In 1810, the census was expanded to obtain information on manufacturing quantity and value. In 1850, taxation, churches, pauperism and crime were added to the number of variables considered.[14]

The dawn of the Twentieth Century also witnessed further improvements on the American economy. The Civil War had ended, there had been an upsurge of inventions; cars were replacing carriages; airplanes were increasingly becoming an important means of transportation; and Hawaii (1898), Puerto Rico (1898), and the Panama Canal (1904) were now under US jurisdiction. The structural changes in the economy were far-reaching, and government officials and businesses needed more frequent and accurate information about economic indicators. To meet the growing demand for accurate information, the BC was made permanent by an act of Congress in 1902; thereby replacing the temporary census office established for the purpose of decennial enumeration. In 1903, the Bureau moved from the Department of the Interior to the Department of Commerce, and has since continued with the Department of Commerce.

Data on retail sales are heavily focused on transactions involving goods rather than services, and is provided on a monthly basis in a user-friendly time series Excel format. Sales data are seasonally adjusted to correct for seasonal, holiday and trading differences, but not for price changes. Data could also be obtained for annual retail sales.

The BC data are classified into various types of businesses in millions of dollars. These include: (i) motor vehicle and parts dealers; (ii) furniture and home furnishing; (iii) building material garden/supply dealers; (iv) grocery stores; (v) gasoline stations; (vi) sporting goods, hobby, book and music; (vii) department stores; (viii) nonstore retailers; (ix) electronics and appliances stores; (x) food and beverage stores; (xi) health and personal stores; (xii) clothing and accessory stores; (xiii) general merchandise stores; (xiv) foodservice and drinking places; and (xv) miscellaneous stores retailers.

Early reports of retail sales are normally based on surveys which give an approximation of consumer spending. The final reports are therefore more substantial or meaningful for econometric or statistical analysis. Dollar amounts are compiled after returns by customers and various taxes are excluded as well as finance charges from department store credit cards.[15]

Chicago Board of Trade (CBOT)[16]

The Chicago Board of Trade was founded by 82 Chicago merchants in 1848 to satisfy the need for a central market place. The market which was originally intended to be a forward/derivative market for the buying and selling of agricultural products, makes provision for a diversified array of commodities today which include precious metals, US and foreign government securities, US and foreign stock indices, and mortgage-backed securities.

The now prominent concepts of "futures contract" and performance bonds, otherwise known as "margins," were formalized in 1865 as grain trading developed standardized agreements. The Great Chicago Fire of 1871 incinerated the home and records of the CBOT, but it was able to reopen two weeks after the fire. In the 1870s futures trading became more formalized, and businessmen in search of fortune were able to become a class of speculators. Speculators in the derivative market have no inherent cash market exposure, in the sense that as buyers or sellers, they do not have ownership of a commodity to be transferred which is subject to risks. They participate in market transactions with the specific objective of making profit.

Like the NYSE, the CBOT is merely a facilitator of trade with stringent rules of operations or engagement in trade. It does not buy or sell commodities and it is regulated by law. The Board sets the following as some of its important objectives: (i) protecting market users and the public from fraud, manipulation and abusive practices; (ii) fostering open, competitive and financially sound futures and options markets; (iii) ensuring principles of justice and equity in trade; and (iv) acquiring and disseminating valuable commercial and economic information. It is also expected to respond to requests filed under the Freedom of Information Act.

Regulation of the CBOT is not a new phenomenon. For example, in 1922, the federal government establishes the Grain Futures Administration to regulate grain trading, and today it is regulated under the Commodity Futures Modernization Act (CFMA, 2000), enforced by the Commodity Futures Trading Commission (CFTC). Regulation ensures price discovery, whereby future market prices are revealed through the trading of futures contracts. Regulation ensures the offsetting of inordinate risks that could otherwise be attributed to adverse or whimsical price gyrations in the derivative market. Risks are of two varieties: (i) price risk, which is a variation in the general market price level in the futures market; and (ii) basis risk, which is a deviation of the futures price from the cash price.

Derivative markets, which are at times confused with typical forward markets, may be seen as markets in which accounts are settled on a daily basis to deal with the expectations of prices at a precise future date in an economic world that lacks perfect foresight. Expectations and speculation provide a leveraged atmosphere for trade which provides liquidity to the markets and enhances the efficiency of its participants.

Expectations are often times significant for economic outcomes, and should not therefore be underrated in the estimation of economic performance. Researchers may therefore make reasonable assumptions about expectations as and when necessary. Such assumptions are normally made feasible by a sense of rationalism, convincing trends, and/or seasonal behavior of markets.

Today, as futures contracts are settled on a daily basis, a safety net is provided to neutralize the risks and probability of default associated with futures contract. To this end, futures exchanges have a clearinghouse to match the buys and sells that take place during the day and to keep track of who owes what to whom—marking-to-the-market, based on margin requirements. The account of each member is therefore settled at the end of each day. On January 3, 2005, CBOT announced that 2004 was the Exchange's most successful year ever with the volume of contracts amounting to nearly 600 million. Total annual volume rose thirty-two percent over the prior year, making 2004 the third consecutive record-breaking year for the CBOT.[17]

The CBOT provides free quotes, online interactive and archived seminars, tutorials, and historical data. Historical market data could be classified under the following broad headings: (i) agricultural products; (ii) financial products; (iii) equity index products; and (iv) metal products.

Data on agricultural products are available for corn, soybeans, soybean oil, wheat, oats, rough rice, and Dow Jones AIG commodity index. Information on financial products include: thirty year bonds (the US government stopped issuing these on October 31, 2001); five and ten year notes; thirty day Fed Funds and ten-year Muni Note Index. Data are also available on equity index products, specifically mini-sized Dow ($5) and Dow Jones Industrial Average ($10); and metal products of gold and silver.

National Association of Securities Dealers Automated Quotation System (NASDQ); American Stock Exchange (AMEX); and Yahoo Finance[18]

Not all securities are sold in organized secondary markets. Markets which are not very well organized are generally referred to as over the counter (OTC) markets. These markets do not normally have very stringent conditions, as those of the organized markets, and use much less traditional/conservative methods, like the telephone, computer networking, and negotiations to transact business. The networking potential has even encouraged firms who are qualified to do business in organized exchanges to stay in the OTC markets.

Trading in the organized NYSE, requires the ability to meet baseline prerequisites, which might not be attained by all traders of secondary securities, and is usually done by outcry or auction. Prerequisites for trading in organized market include a required minimum number of holders of round lots, and a stipulated value of publicly owned shares, annual earnings, and net tangible assets. NASD has similar prerequisites and more, which are less stringent.

The NASDQ is a product of an association of securities brokers and dealers organized after the passage of the Maloney Act in June of 1938, which first considered itself the National Association of Securities Dealers (NASD). In fact the Maloney Act could also be considered as the Maloney Amendment, because it was designed to amend the Securities Exchange Act of 1934 to regulate the OTC markets through the Securities and Exchange Commission (SEC).

The Great Depression demonstrated an urgent need for transparency in investment, but as law makers tried feverishly to forestall another depression by the passage of the National Industrial Recovery Act (NRA), the Supreme Court of the US pronounced the NRA unconstitutional in 1935. To ensure confidence and high ethical standards, the NASD then took upon itself an important objective of regulating itself voluntarily.

The association lists as some of its most important objectives, the standardization of principles and practices to promote high standards of commercial honor among its members; the adoption, administration, and enforcement of rules of fair practices to promote just and equitable principles of trade to protect investors; and the promotion of self-discipline among its members, and the resolution of disputes between its members, and its members and the investing public.

The association is empowered to inspect members' books and records to ascertain if rules have been or are being violated and random examinations are conducted with or without complaints to check on the performance of its members. In enforcing the NASDQ's Code of Fair Practice, registered employees of members of the NASDQ are also subject to investigations and checks.

The system of automated quotation for OTC securities became operational in February of 1971, providing minute by minute bid-ask quotations on OTC securities. OTC trading became very transparent and highly centralized, thereby supplanting the previous system of complete decentralization among broker-dealer firms trading OTC securities. One of the most remarkable changes in the 1971 development, was the increased efficiency with which a broker could obtain the best bid-ask prices; where "ask" is the selling price, and "bid" is the buying price. The probability of trading on the best available prices was greatly enhanced by the 1971 development.

In October of 1998 the American Stock Exchange (AMEX), merged with NASDQ to become a subsidiary of NASDQ. The combination provides an opportunity for a single organization to bring together products of the largest nonfinancial companies.

More than 100 vendors are authorized to distribute real time NASDQ and AMEX market data to the public. Vendors use a variety of communication services to release market data. Such methods involve dedicated computer terminals, data feeds, pagers, and the Internet.

Yahoo Finance provides comprehensive time series historical data on the DOW, NASDAQ, Standard and Poor (S&P) 500, 10-year Bond, NYSE, and NASDQ volumes of trade. The interactive provision allows researchers to select intervals of data (i.e.) daily, weekly, or monthly; or dividends only as well as specific companies of interest. Researchers also have the option of selecting a base year. Yahoo Finance is highly user-friendly. Query is instantly and conveniently downloaded into Excel spread sheet if desired for econometric or statistical analysis.

Data on opening, high, low, and closing prices; and average volume of trade together with adjusted closing prices (i.e.) prices adjusted for dividends and splits are reported. Splits are reported as increases in a corporation's number of outstanding shares of stock without change in shareholders' equity or aggregate market value at the time of the split—increases in shares which cause a corresponding drop in price per share.

The University of Michigan's Consumer Sentiment Index[19]

Since the mid 1940s the University of Michigan has been gauging consumer attitudes on business climate, personal finance and shopping attitude. In actual fact business climate, personal finance and shopping attitude are the central components of the sentiment index. The rational behind the sentiment index is to be able to come up with a method of quantifying consumer expectation and predicting consumer behavior based on rational analysis. Indices of such nature attempt to deal with the volatility of human behavior in order to make predictions. Because it makes economic sense to be able to make projections or forecast the behavior of economic agents, it is essential that a methodology be developed to identify potential behavior. It is believed that sentiments are normally very telling. For example, consumers with a very somber mood, who are also very concerned about their finances, are not generally prone to go on a shopping spree. Consumers are predominantly seen as risk averse and more sensitive to losing money. Therefore businesses would tend to do well if they could factor the consumer temperament of the times in making plans for the future. For example they must start thinking about cost or profit potential, as much as the ramifications of accumulating or reducing inventories based on potential sales.

The Consumer Sentiment Index is in reality based on consumer thinking about current situation (current finances and buying plans) and expectations of the future five years. Data are collected up to a day or two before the official release on the last Friday of every month.

The spending behaviors of consumers reflect their perception of economic variables such as inflation, interest rates, and oil prices. For example, the looming concern over increasing oil prices in the first quarter of 2005 contributed to a drop of the Sentiment Index. Oil prices have the potential of seriously weakening the financial situation of consumers. By the end of the second quarter of 2005 buying attitudes toward vehicle dropped as a result of the uncertainty of oil prices.

The Sentiment Index reports a monthly decomposition of its core indicators. These include the expected change of: current financial situation; interest rate; unemployment; income; and opinions about government economic policies. The gyrations of consumer sentiments, which may or may not lead to self-fulfilling prophecy, for better or worse, are of keen interest to brokerage firms, lenders and retailers who are willing to subscribe to such surveys in order to stay one step ahead. The net result is that these indices provide a barometer to measure the temper of the times and to predict the direction of the economy.

The World Bank/International Bank for Reconstruction and Development (IBRD)[19]

The World Bank has two important comprehensive data compilations— World Development Indicator (WDI), and Global Development Finance (GDF). Knowledge of the performance of international economies and international economics is crucial to fast-pace or high performance businesses and international investors. In fact a lot of foreign investors pay very close attention to warning indicators of risk before they venture capital into countries. This is certainly not an unreasonable undertaking.

Today the global economy is thoroughly integrated and economies have become greatly interdependent. Nations trade with one another and therefore need knowledge about their trading partners (the trading environment), the level of development, as well as methods of financing trade. They also need critical information about economic indicators on which to make decisions.

The International Bank for Reconstruction and Development (IBRD)/World Bank is not an agent for financing trade or correcting temporary balance of trade disequilibrium as is the International Monetary Fund (IMF). The World Bank takes on a broader initiative which is to foster and maintain development. This also entails, by definition, assistance with structural changes geared toward development. It is in reality a specialized agency of the United Nations (UN), rather than an example of a traditional or perceived common place bank.

The World Bank came into being in December 1945, after twenty-eight countries ratified the Bretton Woods Agreements in 1944. The Bank is made up of three separate institutions—the IBRD, the International Development Association (IDA), and the International Finance Corporation (IFC).

The IDA was established in 1960 as part of the World Bank Group that provides long-term interest-free loans (credits) and grants to the poorest of the developing countries to support economic growth, reduce poverty and improve living conditions. Relative poverty, at the time of this writing, is defined as per capita Gross National Income (GNI) of US $865 per year. IDA loans are intended to offset the inability of low-income countries to borrow money in international markets, or to do so at high interest rates.

The IFC was founded in 1956 as a source of loan and equity financing for private sector projects in the developing countries. The Bank has since its inception, become the largest multilateral source of funds for development, and lending to needy countries has progressively increased over the years.

The common goal of the Bank's component parts is to help raise the standards of living in developing countries by providing financial resources from developed countries to the developing. The Bank supports efforts of developing countries to build schools and health centers, provide water and electricity, fight disease and protect the environment.

Use of the Bank's resources or funds is highly contingent on the satisfaction of basic rules, including the following: (i) loans must be made to governments, or guaranteed by governments; (ii) rate of interests must be consistent with prevailing rates in the world's money market; (iii) repayment is expected within ten to thirty-five years (with some exceptions for concessional loans); (iv) that provision be made for an investigation into the probability of repayment, partly based on the soundness of the project and financial responsibility of the government; and (v) surveillance of the intended project by the Bank to ensure proper execution and management. The Bank conducts research and provides technical assistance, and coordinates assistance from a variety of sources to individual countries.

Both the WDI and GDF contain data that generally rely on official sources, although by its admission, the Bank makes some adjustments to the balance of payments to account for fiscal/calendar-year differences. The Bank makes an effort to present data that are consistent in definition, timing and methods, although revisions may show discrepancies in editions. The data are exceedingly friendly with Excel and provision is readily available to export a query from the Bank's database online or on CD-ROM to Excel. Data are provided for various categories of countries (i.e.) in aggregates, based on income; level of indebtedness; and geographic region; as well as for individual countries.

The low, middle and high income categorization are based on the Banks operational lending categories. The 184 member countries and other countries with populations of more than 30,000 (totaling 208) are classified into groups. Income classification generally reflects the level of per capita GNI.

Indebtedness is reported in three forms: (i) severely indebted (present value of debt service to GNI of 80 percent, and a present value of debt service to exports of 220 percent, based on Debtor Reporting System, DRS); (ii) moderately indebted (key ratios exceed 60 percent but are less than critical levels, based on DRS); and (iii) less indebted. Geographic region data are reported for low- and middle-income economies only.

The WDI is the Bank's "premier annual compilation about development". The 2004 compilation includes approximately 800 indicators and 87 tables. The tables cover 152 economies and 14 country groups. The WDI CD-ROM or WDI online provides time-series data from 1960.

Data are provided for, and not restricted to the following: (i) agriculture; (ii) aid; (iii) debt; (iv) finance; (v) GDP/GNI; (vi) private sector (proceeds, stock market, and FDI); (vii) poverty; (viii) purchasing power parity; (ix) industry; (x) population; (xi) trade; and (xii) governance (corruption and transparency).

On an annual basis, the World Bank provides a review of recent trends and prospects for financial flows to developing countries. The review highlights potential vulnerability associated with private flows—interest rates in advanced economies; volatility of exchange rates and financial markets, attributable to current account imbalances; and apprehension over policy slippages in macroeconomic management in developing countries.

The GDF provides data for 136 countries that report under the Bank's DRS, and data for regions and income groups. It also provides data for total external debt stocks and flows, aggregates, and key debt ratios, and information on the debt of individual countries. The GDF provides more than 200 historical time series going back to 1970, and much more recently, data for group estimates. "By providing a comprehensive review of recent trends in and prospects for all development-related flows (including debt, equity, official aid, and workers' remittances), Global Development Finance...enables government officials, economists, investors, financial consultants, academics, and policymakers in the development community to better understand, manage, and promote the key challenge of financing development in today's globalized environment."[20]

The International Monetary Fund (IMF)[21]

The IMF, like the World Bank, is a specialized agency of the UN. The premier data compilation of the IMF is the International Financial Statistics (IFS). The primary objectives of the IMF are to promote: international monetary cooperation, exchange rate stability, economic growth, and balance of payments equilibrium. These goals are not often, easily obtainable.

The IMF is the product of a Bretton Woods conference in New Hampshire of the US in July 1944. The 45 governments who were represented in that conference sought to erect a structure that would forestall the financial calamities of the 1920s and 30s. The financial turbulence which preceded the convocation of the conference was largely attributed to competitive devaluation (a beggar-thy-neighbor trade strategy), the adverse consequences of global warfare, and the sudden loss of confidence in financial markets.

International trade and employment are key features of international relations and economic growth. When they are severely hampered, a situation of stagnation or recession becomes highly probable. To address this situation, the IMF provides a framework within which international payments and the exchange rate of assorted currencies could foster international trade rather than stifle it. When trade becomes an engine of economic growth, the probability of alleviating or reducing poverty increases tremendously.

To promote economic growth with the hope of reducing poverty, and vulnerability to financial crisis, the IMF advises and assists member countries in implementing economic and financial policies. The preoccupation with the avoidance of crisis is grounded on the idea that financial crisis destroys the potential of creating jobs, reduces income, and exacerbates human suffering. In a globally integrated world, crisis could be contagious rather than isolated. The consequences therefore transcend national frontiers; particularly for large open economies.

The IMF believes that the attainment of economic progress and stability involves good governance; building strong financial and economic institutions; following sound macroeconomic (fiscal, monetary, and exchange rate) policies; and collecting, monitoring and disseminating high quality data.[22] The IMF uses surveillance (oversight of economic policies of its members); technical assistance (advice and training on a range of institutional and policy issues); and lending (financial assistance when a member experiences balance of payments difficulties associated with exogenous, or undesirable shocks which threaten financial stability).

The Statistics Department of the IMF makes its database available to subscribers via CD-ROM or online service. The IFS database contains time series data since 1948 and is highly user-friendly. Its interactive and spreadsheet capabilities allow the researcher to select variables of interest, the query/result of which could be promptly exported into Excel for statistical or econometric analyses.

The IFS database contains approximately 32,000 time series covering more than 200 countries. The IFS is a standard source of international statistics on all aspects of international and domestic finance. "It reports, for most countries of the world, current data needed in the analysis of problems of international payments and of inflation and deflation (i.e.) data on exchange rates, international liquidity, international banking, money and banking, interest rates, prices, production, international transactions, government accounts, and national accounts."[23] The exchange rate for all Fund member countries, Aruba, and Netherlands Antilles is provided.

Transparency International (TI)[24]

TI has earned a reputation as one of the leading compilers of data on corruption. The organization is an international non-governmental organization which is devoted to combating corruption, promoting civil society, and bringing governments together to fight corruption and promote international business. Through its international Secretariat and more than 85 independent national chapters around the world, the organization is committed to fighting the supply of, and demand for corruption. To this end, TI focuses on the prevention of corruption and the reforming of bureaucratic systems.

TI was launched in May 1993 by a group of ten individuals who were concerned about the detrimental effects of the corrupt alliance of bureaucrats and businessmen across international frontiers. The formation was largely conceived on the idea that corrupt practices have undesirable effects on human rights and sustainable development (which also involves use of the environment). The key was to focus on the mechanics behind the conduct of export activities in developing countries and the role of the private sector. It was discovered that the private sector contributed significantly to the undermining of governance in the developing world and countries in transition.

Today, corruption has taken a global dimension of serious concern in the conduct of international business. Corruption is largely seen as a legal wrong which arises from a particular conduct or activity, and is usually suggestive of moral depravity on the part of individuals, bureaucrats or businesses. In much more lucid or precise terms, it could be seen as the abuse of public office for private gain which elicits understandable repugnance.

Corruption is generally indicative of a lack of business ethics, and is often times reckoned with surreptitious or nontransparent/opaque behavior. Drabek and Payne (2001) describe nontransparency from an international perspective, as a set of government policies that increase the risk and uncertainty faced by economic actors or foreign investors. It should be pointed out that the lack of transparency could be otherwise understood as the lack of predictable enforcement of policies or rules as a result of bribery and corruption.

The issue of corruption is obviously not an entirely new concept. As a matter of research and policy it has gained increasing prominence since the 1960s. In the 1970s the US Congress prohibited American individuals and corporations from bribing foreign government officials by passing the Foreign Corrupt Practices Act of 1977. The legislation imposed tax penalties, fines and prison terms for executives of American companies that pay bribes.

Over the years the debates on corruption have intensified, and have largely focused on two diametrically opposed concepts/questions: (i) does corruption impede the flow of investment?; and (ii) does corruption hasten the flow of investment by cutting through bureaucratic red tape? Of course there are macroeconomic issues that could be related to the issue of corruption. For example, does corruption affect development and growth? Does investment in human capital reduce corruption? The ethical issue is unequivocal. Corruption is unethical. What seems to be largely equivocal is the amount of investment that could be associated with corruption or other non-related corruption factors like market size and human capital. It is worth noting that countries which are perceived of as highly corrupt are also capable of attracting substantial amounts of investments although investors are greatly concerned about the intensity of corruption. I have called this conundrum "the corruption paradox" elsewhere.

TI currently provides a Corruption Perception Index (CPI), which is a measure of the level of perceived corruption by businesses and financial journalists in about 146 countries. The methodology of indexing perception of corruption has evolved ever since the first issue in 1995; at least in terms of the number of surveys which have been issued. Some have worried that this might distort the perceived level of corruption. But for nine years—1995-2004, the index shows no substantial volatility in the rankings of countries.

The CPI ranks countries on a scale of 0-10; where 0 could be perceived of as pervasive or absolute corruption for business transactions and 10 is symbolic of virtual transparency of business transactions which impact commercial life. Pervasive corruption is indicative of prevalent kickbacks, extortion, incoherent rule adjudication, and/or subversion of rules or laws to compensate investors for the bribery of officials holding public office.

Exercises on data Sources

1. Identify some of the most important criteria for obtaining data. Suppose you are interested in collecting data on US Federal Funds Rate. Identify some of the most important sources of information. What problems are you likely to encounter?

2. Name some of the sources from which you can obtain information about the closing price of stocks for more than thirty years. How do your sources compare with other sources dealing with futures prices in terms of revision, missing values, and difficulty of access? Which sources are more credible?

3. Compare and contrast the rates of inflation for any three states in the United States for the past thirty years. What is the relationship between the rates of inflation, national savings, and unemployment for these years?

4. Compare the income of males and females in any profession or generally for the past thirty years. Using Excel, Eviews or any other software, plot your results. What do your results show? Why do you think there are differences if any?

5. What has been the relationship between the minimum wage and teenage employment in any state or country of your choice for the past thirty years or more? Plot the data you have used to examine the relationship. What conclusions would you make based on your findings? Can you find a similar relationship between total unemployment and real Gross Domestic Product (GDP)?

6. Collect data on the sale of any product for at least thirty years. What has been happening to sales for the period you have considered? Plot the graph for the sales. Describe your data. Is there any seasonality?

7. What factors would you use to measure consumer confidence? Explain how the factors you have considered would relate to the indices of any two organizations or institutions.

8. Suppose you are a sole proprietor who is contemplating selling more of your products to Mexico, China or any foreign country: explain how demand, wages, foreign direct investment, and corruption for the past 20 years would influence your decision.

9. Select any two companies and collect data on the dividend payments made by those companies for the past ten or more years. Which company outperformed the other? Explain why your findings might or might not influence your decision to be a shareholder of any of those companies.

CHAPTER 3

FORECASTING

Individuals and businesses show keen interest in knowing the future for obvious reasons. Individuals would like to maximize utility today and in the future when they get old. Businesses would like to maximize profit today and in the future so that they could continue to grow and make profit. In both situations individuals and businesses could reasonably do so if they could plan ahead very well. Forecasting refers to the act of estimating future events and conditions.

To plan ahead humans (who are also policy makers) encounter three main problems: (i) the lack of supernatural abilities; (ii) the interactive and unpredictable nature of economic variables; and (iii) the unpredictable nature of human behavior. The "Lucas critique" is closely related to the problem of modeling expectations based on observed occurrences and historical data. When conditions change prior observations might not hold and the relationship between variables might not be entirely predictable. To deal with the expectations puzzle, some economists have relied on the concept of rational expectations which is an improvement on the traditional concept of adaptive expectations (expectations based on what transpired in the immediate past).

The concept of rational expectations is predicated on the idea that humans cannot be persistently wrong if they construct their expectations rationally and make projections based on such expectations. Instead of relying solely on past events, rational expectations incorporate all available information. The projections of rational expectations will not be perfect, but the discrepancy between projections and realities could be attributed to random or non-systematic errors. It is actually more of a macro than a micro concept and some macro economists would take exception to the concept.

Monetarists have used the concept to question the inverse relationship between money growth and unemployment. It is argued that economic agents revise their expectations once they have knowledge of the commitment of policy makers to provide solutions to problems; thereby thwarting the perceived goals of policy makers. For example, an increase in the money supply could cause people to revise their expectations about inflation in which case unemployment could not necessarily fall.

On average however, there is no compelling reason why planners should not make projections into the future to manage their affairs prudently based on all available information. Risk taking is also arguably an evident fact of life.

The indices dealt with in the previous chapter are indicative of consumer attitudes which are *prima facie* indicators of the potential behavior of consumers in the future. They provide valuable information which enables businesses and corporations to make future plans about cost and inventories. It must be noted that good forecasts are not perfect foresight, but they provide the best intelligent guesses or projections given an information set.

Firms which want to stay in business and maximize profits or minimize their losses will very much like to make good forecasts about sales and costs by using sound econometric or statistic techniques. Indeed there are various forecasting methodologies to meet specific individual or business objectives. Yet the ultimate goal of all forecasts is to be as accurate as possible; which means making very little error since forecasts are seldom perfect.

The prime indicators of a very good or bad forecast are usually the root mean square error (RMSE) and the Theil's U-statistic which scales the RMSE so that it lies between 0 and 1; where 0 is normally indicative of a perfect match between forecast and actual values and 1 being a very poor match. The ideal situation is therefore to hope for a Theil which is very close to 0. Since the resulting statistics are a product of data, the importance of having accurate or reliable data should be emphasized once more. Good software packages like Eviews report the evaluating statistical results of a forecast in a table.

Stationary and Nonstationary Series

Forecasting could be done with stationary and non-stationary data or series. A series is said to be stationary if its mean and variance are constant over time and if the covariance/autocovariance between time periods depends only on the time lag and not the actual time at which the covariance is calculated. For example, a series starting from 1960 to 2000 should have a consistent mean, variance, and autocovariance even if the commencement of the series is changed from 1960 to 1965. The mean, variance, and autocovariance would then be said to be time invariant. A stationary series exhibit a mean reverting tendency (i.e.) the time series will tend to return to its mean and fluctuations around the mean (variance) will largely show constant amplitude. A non-stationary series does not exhibit such qualities of constancy but could be made stationary by differencing the data.

Differencing is the method of removing the trend from a data when the series is not stationary. This implies that a trend may or may not be stationary. The use of correlograms (the plot of autocorrelation coefficients against lag lengths) is usually a preliminary method of detecting stationarity, by studying the shape of the resulting spikes and their probability value. The trend/secular trend is just one of four components of a time series; the others being cyclical variation; seasonal variation; and irregular variation.

The trend of a time series is the smooth long-term direction of the series. The Dow Jones Industrial Average (DJIA, Figure 3.1) monthly closing price for the period January 3, 2000 to January 3, 2005 shows volatility clustering which is typical of financial series, as well as trends and cycles. "Volatility clustering" is a financial expression for the variance of returns which are high and low for extended periods of time (a form of heteroskedasticity).

A closer look at the graph (Figure 3.1) indicates that between January 3, 2000 and May 2002, the monthly closing price trended downwards and thereafter, upwards. Trends show general direction of the series. It could also be seen that there are evident peaks and troughs over periods which are longer than one year. These peaks and troughs are indicative of cyclical variation.

Figure 3.1: Dow Jones Industrial Average: Price of Last Reported Monthly Trade January 3, 2000 to January 3, 2005 (US$)

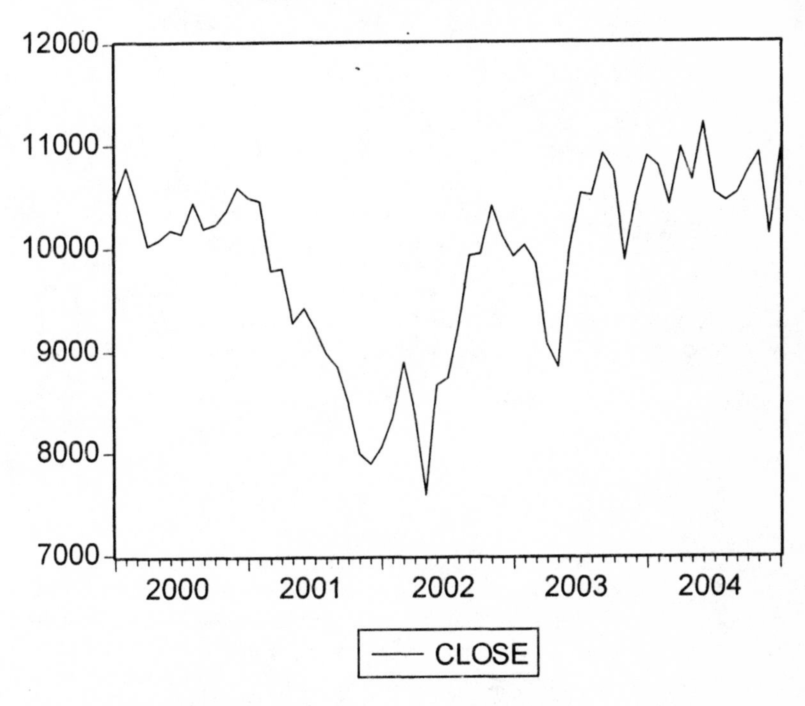

Data Source: Yahoo Finance
Eviews plot of DJIA closing monthly prices, January 3, 2000- January 3, 2005

The Federal Funds Rate (FFR, Figure 3.2); which is the cost of borrowing immediately available funds overnight; also shows an upward trend for the period of June 2004 to March 2005. The effective rate is the weighted average of the reported rates at which different amounts of the day's trading through New York brokers occurs. The FFR mirrors available reserves in the banking system which influences commercial banks' decisions on making loans to deficit spending units (DSUs).

Figure 3.2: Monthly Federal Funds Rate (FFR): June 2004-March 2005 (Percent)

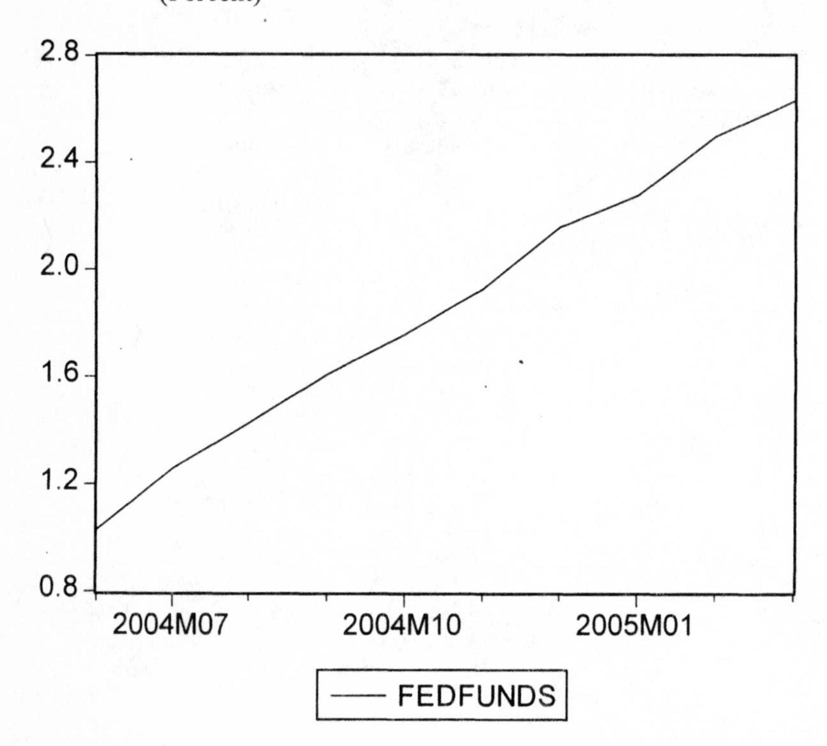

Data Source: Federal Reserve Board of Governors
Eviews plot of FFR, June 2004-March 2005

Time series data may also show seasonality. Patterns of change in time series which repeat themselves every year are considered to be seasonal. For example, one would expect the sales to peak every December, or the demand for snow ploughs to increase every fourth quarter in the US. In general people would actually go on a shopping or spending spree during Christmas time every year.

Since this binge is repeated every year just at about Christmas time, it becomes a seasonal occurrence. Figure 3.3 captures this seasonal pattern.

The total retail and food services sales, excluding motor vehicle and parts for the period January 2001 to December 2004 are plotted in Figure 3.3. It could be clearly seen that in December (at the end of each year) total sales would peak but would drop precipitously in January and then rise again just about the middle of every year when consumers have possibly recovered from debts or dissaving. Consumers also tend to be excited about spring and summer (in geographically affected areas) after a long or stifling winter. It is also evident from Figure 3.3 that there is an upward trend in the total retail sales over time.

This pattern of the data is reflected in the sales of almost all major businesses. It is normal for clothing and toy sales to increase substantially at the end of December each year when Santa is in town.

Figure 3.3: Total Retail and Food Services Sales, Excluding Motor Vehicle and Parts January 2001-December 2004 ($ millions)

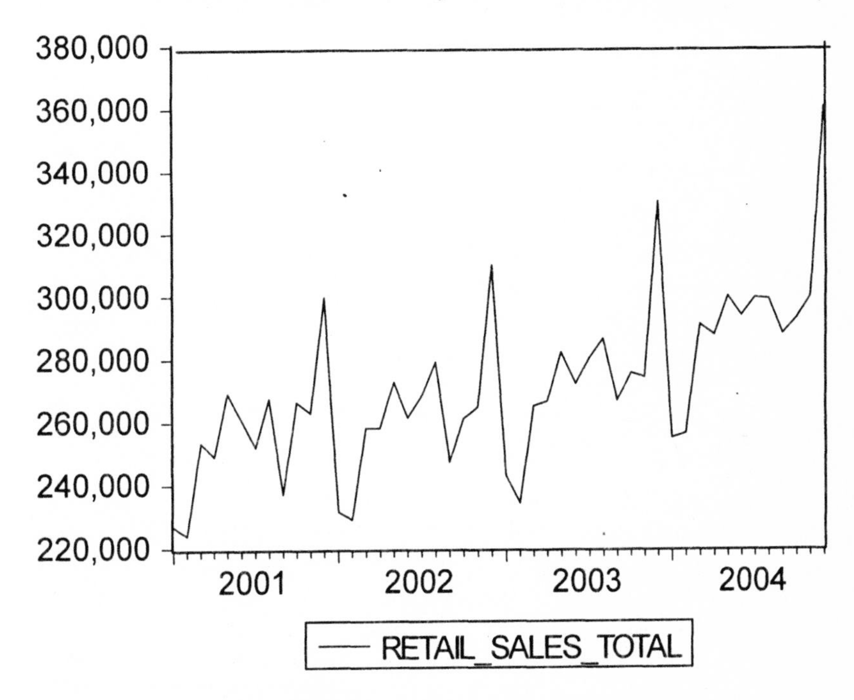

Data Source: US Census Bureau
Eviews plot of Total Retail Sales, January 2001- December 2004

Time series may also show irregular variation which could be classified as episodic and residual/chance. Episodic variations are variations which could be identified but not predicted; for example, natural disasters, or war. The residual is what is left after the episodic impact on the economy has been accounted for.

Regression Analysis and Forecasting

Polling and surveys are sometimes used to make short-term forecasts when quantitative data are not readily available. Because these methods are just as imprecise as regression analysis, it becomes reasonable to use forecasting methods conjunctively or interdependently to obtain a better forecast of variables.[25]

Regression analysis is a method used to establish or explain the relationship between a dependent variable and explanatory variables. Variables are measurable characteristics which take varying numerical values for analysis; for example, 1, 2, 3, 4.... When they are qualitative, (i.e.) not necessarily of numerical values, for example, male, female, black, or white, numerical values could be assigned to their characteristics for distinction, for example 0 if black and 1 if white. This transformation changes the qualitative characteristics into quantitative characteristics known as "dummy variables". Of course a caveat is warranted here. Caution should be exercised in order not to fall into what is regarded as the "dummy variable trap"—a situation in which the number of dummy variables in a regression is set to be equal to the number of characteristics.

If entrapped by dummies, the resulting regression would be spurious or nonsensical because of the inability to isolate the individual effects of the dummies on the dependent variable (multicolinearity); the dummies are highly correlated. The solution is therefore to have one less dummy variable than the relevant dummied characters. For example, instead of having dummies for black, white, and Hispanic (3 dummies), it should be okay to have two dummies 1 for blacks and 0 for others, and 1 for white and zero for others; in symbolic terms, m-1; where m is the number of relevant characteristics.

The dependent variable is normally the variable of interest to forecast or be explained. It is often times referred to by many names—regressand, response variable, endogenous variable, controlled/outcome variable or the predictand. It is usually the variable on the left of a regression equality sign. There are a lot of variables of interest to forecast or explain in Finance and Economics. For example, the consumption of a good, the rate of inflation, gross domestic product, stock prices, average starting salary, interest rate, exchange rates, oil prices, the Dow Jones Index, and the price of agricultural products (especially for the futures market). This is not necessarily an easy task because relevant variables have to be selected to explain these dependent variables.

The variables which are selected to explain the dependent variables are known as the independent variables. Like the dependent variables, they take diverse description—explanatory variables, exogenous variables, predictor variables, control variables, and stimulus variables. These variables are to be found on the right side of the regression equality.

Choosing explanatory variables is not a random matter, but is largely contingent on some kind of theory when a bivariate or multivariate model is preferred. A model is a formal representation of a theory (usually in mathematical form). Bivariate models try to explain the relationship between a dependent variable and an independent variable and a multivariate model uses more than two variables. To see the effect of an explanatory variable on the dependent variable the other explanatory variables are held constant. When the dependent variable is examined over a period of time to make a forecast, the model specification is known as univariate. Time becomes the independent variable.

Model specification is not necessarily a simple matter because a model has to be precise or parsimonious (Ockham's razor) and has to take into consideration the relevant variables without dual/bilateral causality or simultaneity bias (i.e.) the selected dependent variable should not have an effect on the independent variable and vice versa. A common Econometric analogy is to ask the question, what came first, the chicken or the egg? In such a case instrumenting becomes essential in Econometrics. This is a method of using an independent variable or surrogate variable which is correlated with the suspect independent variable but not dependent on the dependent variable. Alternatively, an atheoretic model or method of estimation might be desired with preconditions of stationarity or the absence of unit root. How atheoretic is the model, is subject to debate, but vector autoregression (VAR) is one class of such atheoretic models which is encountered in advance studies of Econometrics. The Box-Jenkins discussed in this chapter is another.

The use of theories is important for economic models because theories are the results of a long drawn out evolutionary process to make generalizations. The first step to developing a theory is to observe real world facts. These facts are then used to develop an unproven but testable assertion of cause and effect explanation known as "hypothesis." Hypotheses are then tested for validity or credibility by comparing the results of other findings so that they could be modified, rejected, or accommodated by a failure to reject. Hypotheses which withstand the grueling test of time ultimately become a theory and subsequently a law or principle as a result of further testing. They consequently form the basis of model specification.

There are a number of important regularity conditions or assumptions which must be made and accounted for when constructing a basic regression model: the model must be linear in the coefficients (numbers which measure characteristics) and correctly specified. If the data does not show a linear relationship, then a quadratic or double log specification is one possibility); provision must be made for an error component which is assumed to be normally distributed with zero population mean and constant variance (homoskedasticity); all explanatory variables are uncorrelated with the error component; explanatory variables must not be a perfect linear function of each other (no perfect multicolinearity); and the error term in one period must not be correlated with the error term of another period (no serial or autocorrelation).

The reason for the observance of these regularity conditions is simply to prevent biased estimation or spurious regression when ordinary least squares (OLS) is used as a method of estimating the coefficients (parameters) of a regression model. The goal is for OLS to be BLUE (Best linear unbiased estimator). The real test of forecasting however is how best to achieve a good forecast with or without unwavering adherence to the totality of the regularity conditions. The goal is almost understandably Machiavellian—the end justifies the means; the end of course being the best forecast.

The ultimate objective of OLS is to minimize the sum of the squared vertical deviations of each point from the regression line. This regression line is otherwise known as the sample regression function (SRF) because a sample is what is realistically dealt with in running a regression. The true population is unobtainable but it is hoped that this line could approximate the population; hence the population regression function (PRF) which is the expectation of how the dependent variable is going to change on average given the expectation of the explanatory variable. The vertical distances between data points and the regression line are the errors which must be minimized or made to be as small as possible. The data points are actual coordinates of the dependent and explanatory variables.

Suppose we are interested in constructing a simple bivariate regression model to explain the relationship between sales and advertising. Imagine further that we are interested only in how advertising affects sales and we are assuming that other variables are not important at this time; for example the price of the product, the price of related commodities, or changes in the income of consumers. How should the inquiry be set up in the form of a regression model? It should be noted that we want to explain the effect of advertising on sales; therefore sales become the dependent variable and advertising the independent variable in this case. This could be written as:

$$\text{sales} = f(\text{advertising}); \qquad (3.1)$$

meaning sales are a function of advertising. The Econometric model will take the form:

$$\text{sales} = a + b^{*}\text{advertising} + e; \qquad (3.2)$$

where a is an intercept parameter—the parameter which tells us the value of sales when there is no advertising taking place; b is a slope parameter—the parameter which tells us by how much sales are going to increase or decrease when advertising goes up or down by a dollar; and e is the error associated with the model which is presumed to be zero. It could therefore be dropped from the equation to be estimated.

Equation 3.2 could otherwise be specified as $Y = a + bX$; the formula for a straight line; where Y is the dependent variable, a is the intercept, b is the slope and X the independent variable. To make the analysis a little bit more lucid consider the advertising example in Dominick Salvatore's Managerial *Economics in a Global Economy.* Assume that the hypothetical data for sales and advertising of a firm, call it XYZ, is the following:

Table 3.1 Advertising Cost and Sales Revenue for Firm XYZ (Millions of dollars)

Year	Advertising	Sales
1991	10	44
1992	9	40
1993	11	42
1994	12	46
1995	11	48
1996	12	52
1997	13	54
1998	13	58
1999	14	56
2000	15	60

Data source: Salvatore's *Managerial Economics in the Global Economy 5th ed.*

A cursory look at the data without any econometric estimation or analysis would reveal that there is a positive correlation between sales and advertising; implying that as the cost of advertising is going up sales are going up. This is symbolic of a positive long-run secular trend.

The results of the regression of sales on advertising are provided by Eviews and reported in Table 3.2. The Eviews analyses can be compared to Salvatore's results. Would the store manager of XYZ be happy with the results of this regression? A few things must be pointed out. At the top of the analysis of variance (ANOVA) (i.e.) the study of the explained sum of squares (ESS) and the residual sum of squares (RSS), Eviews reports the number of observations as "Included observations: 10." This means that 10 observations are considered (1991-2000). Based on the intended motive, there is nothing wrong with this regression, but be aware that a regression purporting to have a normal distribution should have thirty or more observations. Regressions with fewer observations (like the one above) are conventionally considered to follow the *t* distribution.

It is important to take the following from the regression results and interpret them: the R-squared; the advertising coefficient (which prompted the regression to begin with); the standard error associated with the explanatory variable; the t-statistic; the probability of rejecting the t-value; the intercept parameter; and the F-statistic with the accompanying probability of rejection.

The R-squared (coefficient of determination or goodness of fit) is the total amount of variation in the dependent variable (sales) that is explained by variation in the explanatory variable (advertising). In other words it is the ratio of the

Table 3.2 Eviews Result of Table 3 Sales Regression

Dependent Variable: SALES
Method: Least Squares
Date: 04/28/05 Time: 18:59
Sample: 1991 2000
Included observations: 10

Variable	Coefficient	Std. Error	t-Statistic	Prob.
ADVE	3.533333	0.522281	6.765192	0.0001
C	7.600000	6.332324	1.200191	0.2644

R-squared	0.851212	Mean dependent var	50.00000
Adjusted R-squared	0.832614	S.D. dependent var	6.992059
S.E. of regression	2.860653	Akaike info criterion	5.116833
Sum squared resid	65.46667	Schwarz criterion	5.177350
Log likelihood	-23.58417	F-statistic	45.76782
Durbin-Watson stat	1.621113	Prob(F-statistic)	0.000143

explained variation in the dependent variable to the total variation in the dependent variable. In this example, because R-squared is 0.85, 85 percent of the variation in XYZ's sales is explained by the variation in the firm's advertising expenditures. The square root of the R-squared is the correlation coefficient which measures association between sales and advertising rather than variation in sales resulting from variation in advertising.

The advertising coefficient is 3.533333 and the t-statistic is 6.765192 with a probability value of 0.0001. All things being equal (*ceteris paribus*), the manager of XYZ could reasonably conclude with a greater than 95% confidence level that advertising is boosting up sales. This is so because the probability of rejecting his conclusion is less than 5%, and the t-statistic is greater than 2; meaning that the advertising coefficient is significant. It should be pointed out that the ratio of the advertising coefficient to the standard error is the resulting t-statistic—the smaller the standard error, the better the fit. If all the data points were on the regression line, the model will predict sales perfectly. Because they are not, there are errors to be associated with the model which are known as the standard error of the estimate. The standard error estimate measures dispersion around the regression line, just as standard deviation measures dispersion around the mean.

The advertising coefficient suggests that if the firm increases his advertising expenditure by a $1, sales should go up by $3.53 cents. This relationship is normally considered to be the effect on the dependent variable as a result of an incremental (marginal) change in the independent variable for all regression models except arguably the likes of nonstructural VAR which could be made structural anyway. It is important to recognize the sign of the slope coefficient. There are instances when this sign would be negative. In such situations an incremental increase in the explanatory variable leads to a decrease in the dependent variable by the amount of the slope coefficient.

The intercept parameter is defined by *c;* the numerical value of which is 7.6. This parameter suggests that if there is no advertising at all the value of sales would be $7.6 million dollars. The intercept can be calculated by subtracting the product of the slope and the mean of the independent variable from the mean of the dependent variable.[26]

The F-statistic defines the overall explanatory power of an entire regression. In other words it explains how good a regression model is through the ANOVA. The F-statistic is used to test the hypothesis that all regression coefficients are jointly zero. A failure to reject is indicative of the fact that the coefficients are not jointly statistically zero.[27] The F-statistic of the regression is 45.76782 and the probability value is 0.000145. The null that the coefficient is zero is rejected.

Univariate Forecasting

Univariate forecasting is not dependent on theory and should be used more cautiously. The forecaster is barely interested in forecasting the value of a single variable over time without considering other variables that might affect that variable. In such situations time becomes the independent variable (i.e.) time defines the values of the X axis and the variable of interest is the dependent variable (i.e.) the variable on the Y axis.

The values of time are coded or transformed to make for easy and meaningful forecast. Time takes a sequential order of 1, 2, 3, 4…; more specifically, 2006=1; 2007=2; and 2008=3. This will become more apparent shortly. If forecasts are to be credible and reliable, it is generally a good idea to limit the range of forecasts to the very near future and not to a distant future. Two popular suggestions are to limit the forecast period to either $n/2$, or 2 years; where n is the number of forecast observations considered. This is a reasonable caveat for obvious reasons. Over time there is a strong possibility of having all kinds of changes including structural changes. Inflation might soar; unemployment could rise; consumer optimism might change to pessimism; interest rate could rise; or governments could enact unfavorable legislation. These changes would render long drawn dynamic forecasts less.useful or worthless.

It is also a good idea to leave out the last available information to evaluate the accuracy of the forecast. For example, suppose we are interested in predicting sales for 2004 and we have information (data) for 2003. It would be prudent to base our regression model on information till 2002 to first predict 2003. The results could then be compared to the available data for 2003 to evaluate the predictive power of our regression model. We can then forecast two or three years ahead to make decisions about costs, hiring, and trading strategies.

Consider the following practical example. Suppose speculators in the futures market, say the Chicago Board of Trade (CBOT) are interested in forecasting the US production of wheat to make projections about the price of wheat in the future. The futures market, unlike the forward market, is a market in which futures contracts are traded and executed by a clearinghouse on a daily basis rather than at expiration to determine who owes what to whom (marking-to market).

Speculators participate in the market by buying and selling contracts simply to take risks in order to make profits. They have no inherent cash market exposure and they buy futures if they believe prices will rise or sell if they believe prices will fall. Profit realization therefore depends on the differential between expected future prices and actual prices.

The price of wheat is contingent on several factors. For example, foreign production, the cost of fertilizers, weather conditions, prospective global demand and/or supply or even natural disasters as floods. Suppose speculators want to consider those contingencies improbable, or want to hold them constant. How could speculators use univariate forecast to make a determination of the future price of wheat based on the information on the total US production of wheat *ceteris paribus* (other things remaining unchanged)?

Table 3.3 US Wheat Production (Million Bushels)

Year	Total Production (TP)
1967/68	1507.6
1968/69	1556.6
1969/70	1442.7
2070/01	1351.6
.	.
.	.
.	.
2001/02	1947.5
2002/03	1605.9
2003/04	2344.8
2004/05P	2158.2

P= Projected

Source: National Agricultural Statistics Service and Economic Research Service (estimates), USDA.

The primary challenge is to make an intelligent projection, which is perceptibly, a prediction of the total production of wheat. Since the primary interest is in estimating the total production of wheat in the US, the total production of wheat becomes the dependent variable; and time, the independent variable. To enable an assessment of the efficacy of the regression model, the sample could be adjusted to thirty six observations (2002/03) and a one-period/year-ahead forecast could be compared to the known data for 2003/04 in order to evaluate the forecast.

The regression of interest would take the following form:

$$\text{Total production} = a + b^{*}\text{time}; \tag{3.3}$$

Recall that time takes the sequential values of 1, 2, 3.... Simple univariate, bivariate, and multivariate regressions could also be done by Excel and Eviews. Complicating simultaneous regression models would require use of other statistical software. Equation 3.4 gives the forecast result for 2004/5 as follows:

$$\text{TP} = 1750.56 + 18.92(37) = 2450.60 \text{ Million Bushels.} \tag{3.4}$$

This forecast result is clearly not identical to the recorded amount for 2003/4; which is 2344.8 million bushels. In Equation 3.4, a thirty-six-year data is used to do the forecast for the known amount of 2003/4. The amount of 2004/5 is merely a projected amount. The model must therefore be evaluated against its over-predicting capacity of about 4-5 % for the subsequent forecast (i.e.) 2004/5 and beyond. Forecast errors could also be corrected by using Bayesian inferencing techniques (correction based on the inclusion of incremental available data). It should be noted that the forecast is about 95-96% accurate. The forecast result could also be evaluated by the Theil inequality coefficient (0.078) in Figure 3.4. It should be recalled also that the Theil should be very close to zero to get an almost perfect fit. The forecast result of equation 3.4 is based only on the data of wheat production for the past 37 years.

The Theil coefficient can be decomposed into three components (the sum of which must not exceed one): (i) the bias proportion; (ii) the variance proportion; and (iii) the covariance proportion.

The bias proportion tells how far the mean of the forecast is from the mean of the actual series. The variance proportion tells how far the variation of the forecast is from the variation of the actual series; and the covariance proportion captures the remaining unsystematic forecasting errors. A good forecast is usually one for which the bias and variance proportion should be so small that most of the bias would be concentrated on the covariance proportions. The forecast result shows that the US production of wheat is trending upwards; in which case the expected future price could fall in the short-run as a result of an increase in production. Speculators would most likely sell today with the hope of buying tomorrow. If their expectations are realized, they could then make a handsome profit.

Figure 3.4 Result of Eviews Forecast of Regression 3.4

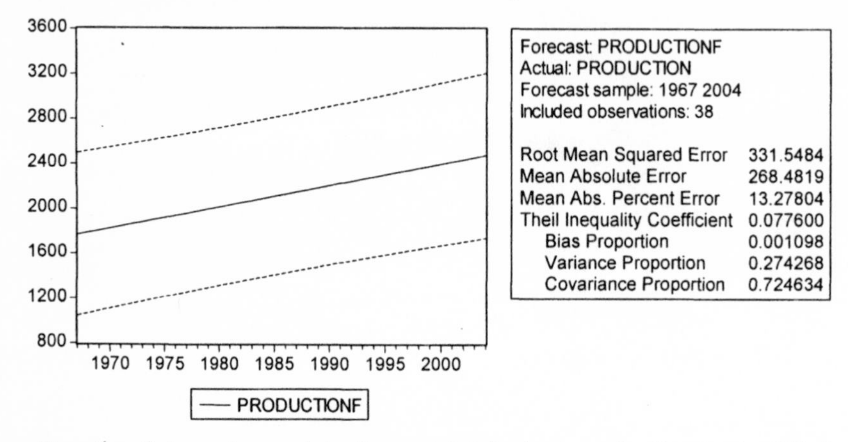

Equation 3.4 can be used to forecast total wheat production in the US for 2004/5 on the condition that there are no significant or structural changes. The forecast equation will take the following form:

$$TP = 1750.56 + 18.92(38) = 2469.52 \text{ Million Bushels.} \tag{3.5}$$

If the forecast is revised downward by about .4%, the forecast result would be approximately 2370.74. This is still slightly higher than the expert projected production. It should however be borne in mind that this is a univariate forecast which has not considered other factors. This does not mean that real production will not be closer or in excess of the predicted amount. A very conservative forecast is intended to accommodate the idea that at some point in time the total US production of wheat will begin to fall as other variables change and become relevant. It will therefore be unreasonable to assume or project that the increase will continue forever.

Bivariate Forecasting

The prefix "uni," means one and "bi" means two. In the previous example we dealt with one variable, hence the word, "univariate." In this section the forecasting approach involves two variables and therefore is bivariate. The fundamental principles of regression analysis remain unchanged, but some kind of theory is subsumed so that the dependent variable is modeled to depend on a particular independent variable of functional interest. Time is no longer the independent variable and actual values of the variables in the model are substituted for time. The forecast is considered to be unconditional when the actual values are known, and conditional, when unknown. The accuracy of the conditional forecast is largely dependent on an unbiased minimum variance forecast of the independent variables. A rule of thumb is to select a variable that is regularly forecasted by experts.

Consider the following two macroeconomic variables of the US economy: the Federal Funds Rate (FFR); and nominal gross domestic product (NGDP). The choice of the two variables is closely related to economic theory involving a monetary policy rule to target nominal GDP (nominal GDP targeting). The Fed announces a planned path for nominal GDP. If nominal GDP rises above the target, the Fed reduces money supply through open market operations (OMO) by selling federal government securities to dampen aggregate demand. OMO involves the freedom to compete in buying and selling federal government securities.

When nominal GDP falls below the target, the Fed increases the money supply by buying federal government securities through the open market to increase aggregate demand. The buying and selling of bonds affect the ability of banks to give out loans based on the level of their liquidity. It is believed that nominal GDP target permits monetary policy to adjust to changes in the velocity of money (the speed at which a dollar is used on average to purchase goods). Therefore targeting nominal GDP would lead to greater stability in output and price than a monetarist policy rule.

The Fed tries to set interest rate such that it could achieve stable prices while avoiding large swings in output and employment Apart from increasing and decreasing the interest rate, there is the question of intensity. How much increase or decrease is warranted? One popular rule is that proposed by John Taylor (Taylor rule), which takes inflation and the GDP gap (the percent by which GDP deviates from its natural rate) into consideration.[28]

The FFR is crucial for a number of reasons. If the Fed is able to influence interest rate successfully it could affect both the goods and money market. The FFR is the "interbank lending rate" which represents the primary cost of short-term loanable funds—the rate banks charge each other for overnight loans to correct their liquidity disequilibrium. Apart from its relevance to monetary policy and measurement on the return of bank reserves, the FFR measures available reserve in the banking system. Available reserves determine how much banks could be able to provide DSUs.

Suppose investors are interested in projecting changes in the FFR in the near future (not an easy thing to do) so that they could make investment decisions today while holding all other variables constant except NGDP. How could investors use bivariate forecasting to make their projection based on information from Table 3.4? It should be pointed out that in reality other factors would be factored into consideration; for example expected inflation rate. Because this is a bivariate example only two variables are considered. The annual rather than the weekly rate is used for convenience to avoid the elaborate data transformation required to make the number of observations for both variables congruent.

Table 3.4 Fed Funds Annual Rate (seasonally unadjusted percent) and US Nominal GDP ($ Billions seasonally adjusted) 1969-2004

Year	Fed Funds Rate	Nominal GDP
1969	8.21	984.6
1970	2.73	1038.5
1971	3.11	1127.1
1972	1.57	1238.3
.	.	.
.	.	.
.	.	.
2001	3.88	10,128.0
2002	1.67	10,487.0
2003	1.13	11,004.0
2004	1.35	11,735.0

Data Sources: Federal Reserve Board of Governors—Fed Funds Rate
US Bureau of Economic Analysis—Nominal GDP

Figure 3.5 shows the graph of Fed Funds Rate and nominal GDP since 1955. After the mid 1980s the data show more of an inverse relationship than a direct relationship when the FFR is compared against time and nominal GDP. The data seems to be partly consistent with the economic theory that there is an inverse relationship between nominal GDP and interest rate. The data shows that this is particularly true for shorter time horizons. The problem of tracking a consistent relationship between FFR and nominal GDP may well be attributed to outside lags; the time it takes for policy to affect the economy. Nominal GDP seems to have a strong explanatory power over the FFR even though other factors, like inflation are equally important.

The regression to be evaluated is of the following form:

$$\text{FFR} = a + b^{*}\text{NGDP} \tag{3.6}$$

It should be noted that in this bivariate or structural form, NGDP has replaced time. The results of equation 3.6 are reported in Table 3.5

The result of the regression is arranged for a comprehensive unconditional forecast in equation 3.7. The coefficient is negative and significant although the amount of explained variation is low as should be expected in this bivariate model. The year 2004 was left out in order to evaluate the effectiveness of the model and the forecast. To forecast FFR for 2004 equation 3.6 is re-written as:

$$\text{FFR} = 10 - 0.000547(11{,}735.0) = 3.6 \tag{3.7}$$

Figure 3.5 Eviews Plot of Federal Funds Rate and Nominal GDP (1955-2003)

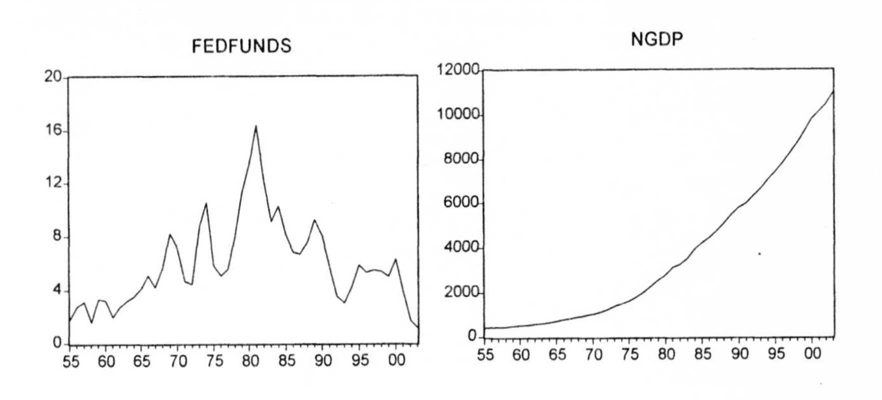

Table 3.5: Regression Result of Equation 3.6

Dependent Variable: FEDFUNDS
Method: Least Squares
Date: 06/03/05 Time: 14:17
Sample: 1969 2003
Included observations: 35

Variable	Coefficient	Std. Error	t-Statistic	Prob.
NGDP	-0.000547	0.000155	-3.540691	0.0012
C	9.657508	0.899036	10.74207	0.0000
R-squared	0.275306	Mean dependent var		6.951429
Adjusted R-squared	0.253346	S.D. dependent var		3.241420
S.E. of regression	2.800883	Akaike info criterion		4.953192
Sum squared resid	258.8832	Schwarz criterion		5.042069
Log likelihood	-84.68085	F-statistic		12.53649
Durbin-Watson stat	0.578913	Prob(F-statistic)		0.001213

The forecast result for 2004 is 3.6 basis point; 3.6 percent.[29] The forecast result evidently overestimated the actual (1.35). The forecast is not however entirely unreasonable. In 2001 the rate was 3.88 and the forecast shows the rate trending downwards which has actually been the case at this writing. It is reasonable to suggest that the reduction is precipitous at least because of the dramatic and sudden structural blow to the US economy when terrorists hit the twin towers in New York on September 11, 2001. This example is a classic case of how things could go wrong with forecasting when there are sudden or unanticipated shocks to an economy. In this case however the dichotomy between the forecasted value and the actual value is not really detrimental if the objective is to project the direction of the interest rate which is actually the objective of this exercise.

As could be expected the Theil inequality coefficient provided in Figure 3.6.

Figure 3.6 Eviews Forecast Result of Equation 3.7 (1969-2004)

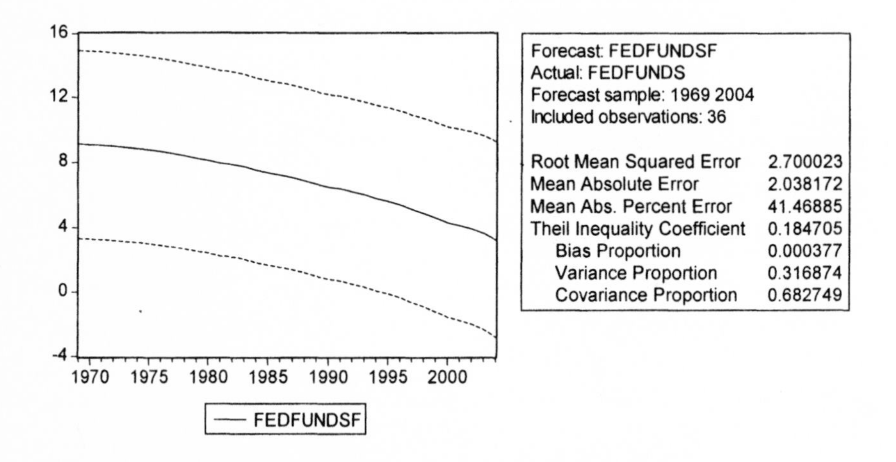

is an interpretation of what the data projects and nothing else. The Theil coefficient is 0.18, with a very low bias and variance proportion.

The FFR forecasting model of equation 3.7 could be used to make a conditional forecast for 2005 when the value of the nominal variable, NGDP is unknown. Professionally estimated values for 2005 could substitute the 2004 value to obtain the 2005 forecast of FFR. Some investors wishing to make profit of bonds could prepare to sell their bonds because bond prices normally rise when interest rate falls. Alternatively investors could make plans to increase investment because of the low cost of borrowing money.

Multivariate Forecasting

Multivariate forecasting is forecasting dealing with three or more variables. As with bivariate forecasting, it is forecasting which is also based on theory. In this example the US exchange rate (the weighted foreign exchange value of the US dollar against the Euro area) is the forecast objective. The explanatory variables include the US consumer price index (CPI), the FFR, and the US balance of payments computed from available statistics provided by the BLS (Table 3.6).

The choice of the variables is largely based on economic theory. The performance of the exchange rate of a nation (the ratio of a domestic currency to foreign currency/currencies) is strongly dependent on a nation's trade with other countries (international trade) and the balance of payments (BOP) gives a summary of all such transactions. Payments made to all other countries are debits and receipts of payments from other countries are credits.

When a nation imports excessively from other countries and/or experiences excessive capital outflows the nation loses reserves (foreign currencies) from its official reserve account which puts an upward pressure on its currency. This causes a chronic balance of payments problem and a depreciation of its local currency. On the contrary if other countries demand more of a nation's goods and services and the nation experiences capital inflows (at times through interest rate adjustments to attract foreign capital), its currency could appreciate if the response is favorable. It should be pointed out that neither excessive appreciation nor excessive depreciation is desirable. The impact of international trade imbalance on the exchange rate could be illustrated by a simple demand and supply analysis. Consider a hypothetical demand and supply analysis of two countries, say US and China in Figure 3.7.

The original equilibrium exchange rate is one for one (i.e.) one dollar ($) for one Chinese Yuan ($\pi$) given by point *A*. At point *A* there is a trade balance. The amount of Chinese goods and services and investment demanded by Americans is equal to the amount of American goods and services and investment demanded by the Chinese and the exchange rate is in equilibrium. If Americans demand an excess of Chinese goods and services as a result of preference for Chinese goods, or experience an outflow as a result of interest rate differential, the original equilibrium defined by point *A* would be disturbed and the original demand curve ($Demand_1$) would shift to $Demand_2$. Without intervention or revaluation, a new exchange rate is now established at point *B* where the new exchange rate is $2/$\pi$1.

The new exchange rate ($2/$\pi$1) is illustrative of a depreciation of the Dollar under the fixed exchange rate system. An extra dollar is required to keep the exchange rate at parity. Americans are now demanding goods and services worth 60 million Chinese Yuan a day at the original exchange rate, causing an excess of 40 million Yuan a day. The Chinese could correct the imbalance by supplying Yuan (40 million a day) through the purchase of US goods (buying

Dollars) or by investing in the US to avoid the appreciation of the Yuan. Alternatively, the US could limit the depreciation if its monetary authority (the Fed)

Figure 3.7 US ($)-China (□) Exchange rate

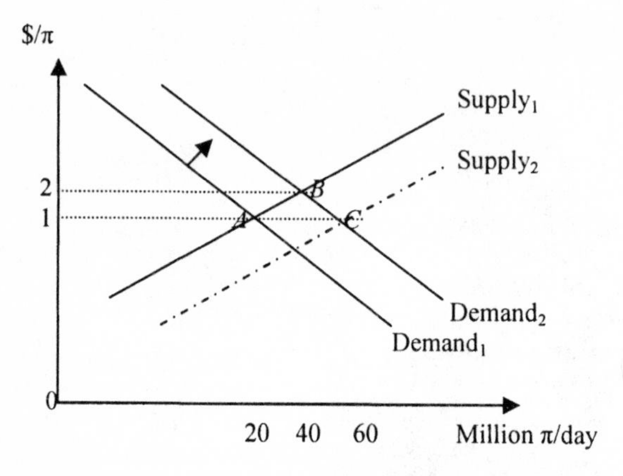

steps in to salvage the exchange rate at a rate in between $1/π1 and $2/π1 (manage/dirty float) or if its monetary authority provides the differential of 40 million Yuan a day from its official Yuan reserves. Under the flexible exchange rate system the demand would be equal to supply and it would be unnecessary to use official reserves of Yuan to correct the imbalance. Theoretically and practically, trade is therefore a very important determinant of the exchange rate.

In close association with trade are the money supply or interest rate and inflation. Currency is normally deposited in another country in order to obtain interest rate. The choice of a country is generally dependent on how high the interest rate is since investors would generally require a higher rate of return on their investments. When money is needed to keep a nation's reserves above a certain level, interest rates are kept high. The opposite is the case when money is not necessarily needed. It should be noted that short-term flows are subject to capital reversibility. The correlation between interest rate and the money supply is a fairly reasonable one to discern.

A decrease in the interest rate which is tantamount to increasing the money supply causes a depreciation of a nation's currency in the long-run. If the economy is close to full capacity, the increase would be inflationary. In the short-run the increase causes a lower interest rate on dollar-denominated securities; bond prices rise; and investors will be unwilling to keep them, except where there is a perception that the local currency will appreciate relative to foreign currencies.

A sustained increase in the general price level (inflation) causes the products of a nation to be expensive relative to others. One of the leading indicators of such price increases is the CPI. When a nation's products become more expensive relative to others, its exports would decline because its products become such price increases is the CPI. When a nation's products become more expensive relative to others, its exports would decline because its products become more costly to purchase. A reduction in exports puts an upward pressure on the local currency causing it to depreciate.

Table 3.6 US Exchange rate (weights for Euro area), Consumer Price Index (CPI, annual city average), FFR, and Balance of Payments (USBOP, $Millions) 1973-2004.

Year	Exchange rate	CPI	FFR	USBOP
1973	21.10	44.4	8.74	2654
1974	20.89	49.3	10.51	2558
1975	20.97	53.8	5.82	-4417
1976	20.80	56.9	5.05	-8955
.	.	.	.	.
.	.	.	.	.
.	.	.	.	.
2001	18.63	177.1	3.88	29307
2002	18.54	179.9	1.67	95028
2003	18.80	184.0	1.13	12012
2004	18.80	188.9	1.35	-51922

Sources: The Federal Reserve Board (exchange rate and FFR) and The US Bureau of Labor Statistics.

The values of the variables provided in Table 3.6 are plotted in Figure 3.8.

The exchange rate (EXCHG) appreciated from 1991-1995; fluctuated for a brief period thereafter; depreciated after 2002 but was fairly stable between 2003 and 2004. The average inflation rate (CPI) progressively increased from 1973-2003. The balance of payments deficit increased precipitously between 1997 and 1998 but was reduced in 1999. The data reflects a halt to the fall in 2001 (the year of the terrorists attack). The multivariate regression model to be estimated takes the form:

$$\text{Exchg} = a + b_1 * \text{CPI} + b_2 * \text{FFR} + b_3 * \text{USBOP} \tag{3.8}$$

The results of the regression are reported in Table 3.7. The Breusch-Godfrey Serial Correlation Test with 2 lags suggests that the errors are not serially correlated (F-stat, 11.23; prob. Value 0.00033). The model is fairly well specified (F-stat: 27.69) and a sufficient amount of the variation in the data (75%) is explained. The signs of the coefficient are as expected; indicating an inverse relationship with the dependent variable. It is particularly striking that inflation stands out as very significant (t-stat of -7.62). Given the regression result, the forecast result for the 2004 exchange rate could be reported as follows:

$$\text{Exchg} = 22.76 + 1.5(10^7)(-51922) + (-0.03)(188.9) + -0.03(1.35) = 16.94 \text{ or } 17 \qquad (3.9)$$

The result of equation 3.9 is fairly close to the actual amount of 18.8 and the Theil Coefficient (0.02) shows a close fit of the actual data and the regression model (Figure 3.9). Therefore the forecast result calls for a slight modification before making a real forecast. In fact the Dollar was pretty stable at 18.8 from 2003 to part of 2005.

Figure 3.8 Eviews Plot of Table 3.6 (1973-2003)

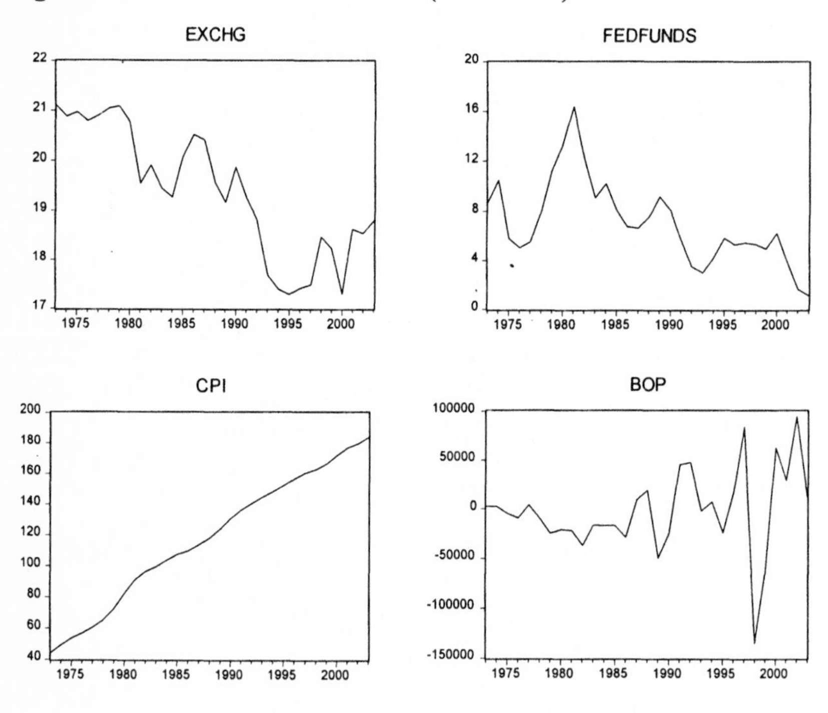

Table 3.7 Eviews Result of Regression 3.8

Dependent Variable: EXCHG
Method: Least Squares
Date: 06/04/05 Time: 16:29
Sample: 1973 2003
Included observations: 31

Variable	Coefficient	Std. Error	t-Statistic	Prob.
FEDFUNDS	-0.027631	0.046947	-0.588548	0.5611
CPI	-0.026980	0.003541	-7.618644	0.0000
BOP	-1.50E-06	3.03E-06	-0.494244	0.6251
C	22.75538	0.673365	33.79351	0.0000

R-squared	0.754727	Mean dependent var	19.37668
Adjusted R-squared	0.727474	S.D. dependent var	1.292287
S.E. of regression	0.674625	Akaike info criterion	2.170595
Sum squared resid	12.28821	Schwarz criterion	2.355626
Log likelihood	-29.64422	F-statistic	27.69381
Durbin-Watson stat	0.657648	Prob(F-statistic)	0.000000

Figure 3.9 Eviews Forecast Result of Regression 3.8 (1995-2003)

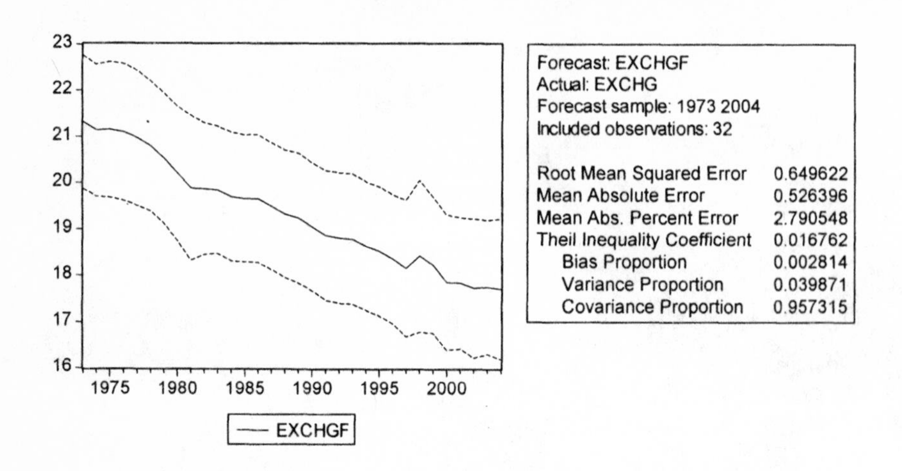

Atheoretic Forecasting with Stationary Data: Box-Jenkins Methodology

This section deals with forecasting which is not necessarily based on theory, and therefore, atheoretic, but for which the data is made stationary. The prior examples are not necessarily based on a stationary data. Time series data which have a clear trend like that of Figure 3.2 do not necessarily have a constant mean and may be nonstationary. In addition to such series many financial series like stock prices exhibit a random walk without a drift time-series process of the form:

$$y_t = y_{t-1} + e_t ; \tag{3.10}$$

where y_t is a dependent variable; y_{t-1} is its lagged value and e_t is a white noise. This process can be made stationary by differencing it once ($y_t - y_{t-1} = \Delta y_t = e_t$), just as other nonstationary series can be differenced for a reasonable amount of time to obtain stationarity. The number of times (d) the integrated process must be differenced to be stationary is generally defined as the order of the integrated process.

An integrated/differenced process is a process consisting of autoregressive (AR) and moving average (MA) processes (ARIMA). An autoregressive model is one for which one of the explanatory variables is a lagged form of the dependent variable (a variable regressed on a past value of itself). This is useful for forecasting a dependent variable based on its past values. The MA model is one for which the time series is regarded as a moving average of a random shock series, e_t. It is typically of the form:

$$Y_t = e_t + \theta\, e_{t-1}; \tag{3.11}$$

where e_t is white noise, and e_{t-1}, its lag. This is other wise considered an MA (1) process.

There are instances, however, in which the dependent variable may not solely be dependent on its past value but on a constant parameter and a moving average of the current and past error terms. In such situations the dependent variable would follow a moving average process. It is also equally plausible for the dependent variable to follow a combination of AR and MA processes; in which case it is said to follow an ARMA process. Moving-averages normally smooth a time series data to see its trend and identify or measure seasonal fluctuations.

In 1976 Box and Jenkins came up with an approach to time series model that may adequately represent the data-generation process for forecasting. The breakthrough was highly suggestive of the model type—AR, MA, or ARMA; and the accompanying order that is consistent with the model selection. They suggested four crucial steps: (i) identification; (ii) estimation; (iii) diagnostic checking; and (iv) forecasting.

The identification process involves the identification of an AR, MA or ARMA process and the required differencing through the use of correlograms. The autocorrelation function (ACF) and the partial autocorrelation function (PACF) which are plotted against corresponding lag lengths indicate significant lags and autocorrelations which inform the modeler about model selection after differencing. The rule of thumb for the selection of lag length is usually a third or a quarter the length of the series. The sample ACF is the ratio of the sample covariance at a particular lag to the sample variance, or the relationship/correlation of a time series and its lags. The PACF removes correlation which could be attributed to intervening variables. In other words it measures the relationship/correlation between two variables which is not explained by the joint relationship of the two in relation to others.

The significance of both the ACF and PACF are determined within a 95% confidence interval. First differencing might not necessarily make the data stationary, for which further differencing may be required. It is important not to difference the data excessively. Once the data is made stationary it is important to check at what lag/s there are significant spikes beyond the confidence limits. Those lags are candidates for model selection. Their coefficients might not be significant in a regression and must therefore be dropped out of the model selection process.

The shapes of the correlograms are more of a guide than a clear cut rule for modeling; implying that individual judgment, trials, and intuition are equally pertinent. The correlogram of a MA process is zero after a point; that of an AR process declines geometrically; and that of an ARMA process shows different patterns (but all dampen after a while).[30]

After the model has been identified, the model could then be estimated by OLS. Estimation requires some amount of vigilance. Insignificant coefficients must be dropped from the model. The R-squared and adjusted R-squared assume the normal interpretation given to OLS regression. They give a *prima facie* indication of the goodness of fit.

Diagnostic checking evaluates the soundness of the model in terms of its reasonable fit to the data. This could be done by analyzing the ACF and PACF of the residuals to see if any is significant. If any is significant the model should be modified. Alternatively, the Q-statistic could be used to test whether all the autocorrelation coefficients are jointly zero. To ascertain that the autocorrelation and partial autocorrelation residuals are random, the Q-statistic must not be significant.

Once a model has been identified, estimated and checked, the model could then be used for forecasting. The Box-Jenkins methodology is well suited for univariate forecasting. Atheoretic multivariate forecasting which might also involve dual causality could be handled by VAR after the data has been made stationary.

Strategies of forecasting which have been discussed, could also be applied to the Box-Jenkins methodology; for example, saving a portion of the data to evaluate the forecast before making any out of sample forecast.

Box-Jenkins Application to the DJIA Monthly Close October 1928 - September 2005

In this section allusion is made to the DJIA monthly close from October 1928 to September 2005. The data show an upward trend (Figure 3.10) which is characteristic of nonstationary series (i.e.) a trend which is not stationary. This is confirmed by the random walk correlogram in Figure 3.11 which shows reasonably high autocorrelation coefficients at lags up to thirty six lags (0.789).

The prime objective becomes differencing the data to achieve stationarity. Eviews permits differencing the data twice. This can be reasonably understood as a safeguard against overdifferencing which causes an increase in the standard deviation or the root mean square error (RMSE). The correct amount of differencing is usually the lowest order which causes a series to fluctuate around a mean value. A noticeable guide to that end is to watch for autocorrelations with negative coefficients or coefficients which are very close to zero. Overdifferencing has a tendency of generating more AR or MA term than might be required. Mild underdifferencing is usually compensated for by adding AR terms, while mild overdifferencing could be compensated for by adding MA terms.[31]

The DJIA data (illustrated in Figure 3.10) is readjusted in order to evaluate model specification before forecasting. The adjusted sample covers January 1930 to June 2004; providing a total of 894 observations. Adjusting the sample provides an opportunity to evaluate the model for subsequent months for which data is available. The data for the adjusted sample is differenced once in order to obtain stationarity and the result is provided in Table 3.8. The inverted roots are stationary. Additionally Eviews provides a warning if the model is not stationary.

The identification process is a combination of art and science but probably more of an art than a science. The trick involves identifying the correct AR, MA, or ARIMA process by differencing and interpreting the resulting correlogram. There has not been a perfect answer to the interpretation of correlograms, but it has become fashionable to rely on certain rules of thumb for model identification; the most important being the avoidance of overdifferencing and underdifferencing (although the damage could be salvaged by adding more AR and MA terms).

The PACF of Figure 3.11 shows no significant spikes at lags 13 and/or 25 to suggest any significant seasonal pattern. It could reasonably be assumed that differencing the data once would suffice to produce the required stationarity.

The DJIA data exhibits symptoms of overdifferencing if it is differenced more than once. The ACF plot at lag 1 is -0.504; a negative spike at lag 1 which is significant (Figure 3.12). A negative ACF coefficient close to 0.5 for this lag is conventionally an indication of overdifferencing. In addition, the signs of the

Figure 3.10: DJIA Monthly close October 1928- May 2005

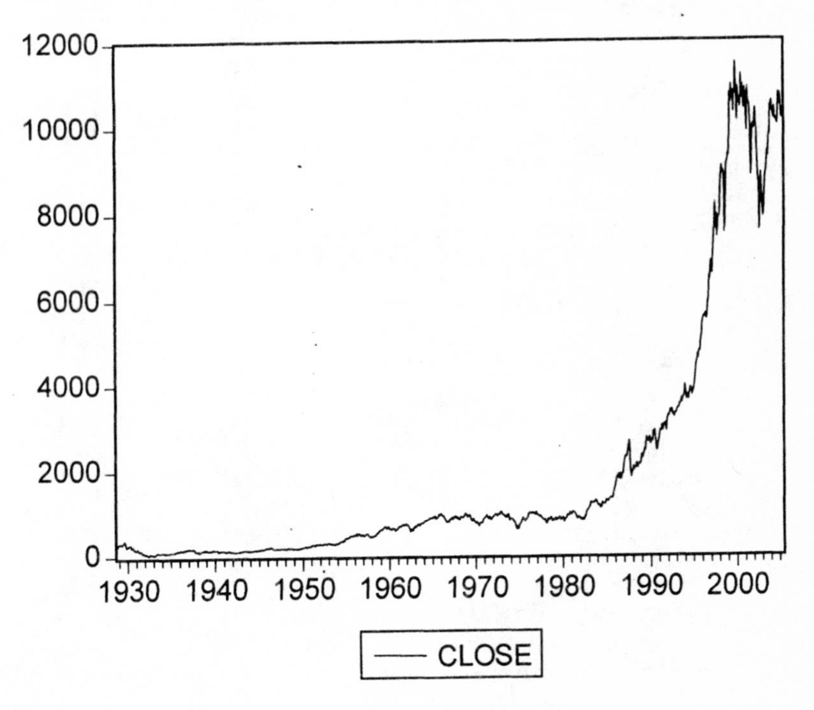

Data Source: Yahoo Finance.

Figure 3.11: Correlogram of DJIA Monthly Close (Level) January 1930 to June 2004

Date: 05/09/05 Time: 10:55
Sample: 1928M10 2005M05
Included observations: 920

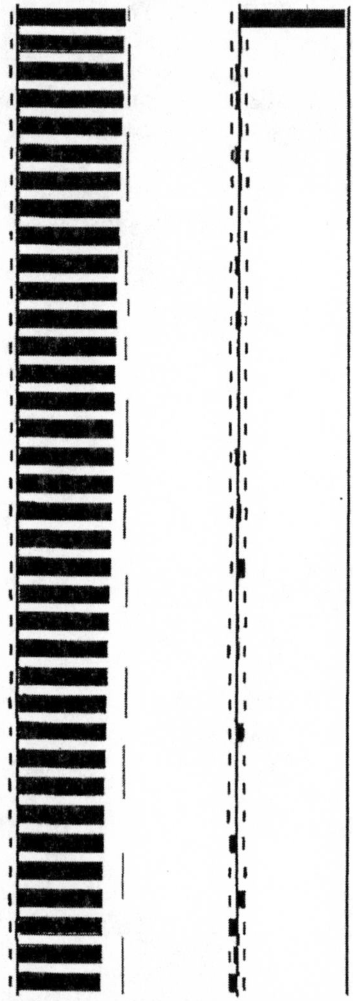

Autocorrelation	Partial Correlation		AC	PAC	Q-Stat	Prob
		1	0.994	0.994	911.60	0.000
		2	0.988	0.023	1813.5	0.000
		3	0.982	-0.021	2705.2	0.000
		4	0.976	-0.022	3586.4	0.000
		5	0.970	0.032	4458.0	0.000
		6	0.963	-0.034	5319.3	0.000
		7	0.957	0.023	6170.9	0.000
		8	0.952	0.014	7013.2	0.000
		9	0.946	-0.006	7846.2	0.000
		10	0.940	-0.027	8669.4	0.000
		11	0.934	0.000	9483.0	0.000
		12	0.927	-0.026	10287.	0.000
		13	0.921	-0.015	11080.	0.000
		14	0.915	-0.005	11863.	0.000
		15	0.908	-0.009	12635.	0.000
		16	0.901	0.003	13398.	0.000
		17	0.895	-0.019	14150.	0.000
		18	0.888	-0.015	14892.	0.000
		19	0.882	0.025	15623.	0.000
		20	0.875	-0.008	16345.	0.000
		21	0.869	0.050	17058.	0.000
		22	0.863	-0.009	17762.	0.000
		23	0.858	0.010	18457.	0.000
		24	0.852	0.023	19145.	0.000
		25	0.847	-0.004	19824.	0.000
		26	0.841	-0.001	20495.	0.000
		27	0.836	0.056	21160.	0.000
		28	0.832	-0.001	21818.	0.000
		29	0.827	-0.012	22468.	0.000
		30	0.822	-0.011	23112.	0.000
		31	0.816	-0.057	23748.	0.000
		32	0.811	0.005	24376.	0.000
		33	0.806	0.078	24997.	0.000
		34	0.801	-0.072	25611.	0.000
		35	0.795	-0.028	26218.	0.000
		36	0.789	-0.065	26815.	0.000

Figure 3.12: Correlogram of DJIA Monthly Close January 1930 to June 2004 (Second Difference)

Date: 05/13/05 Time: 10:03
Sample: 1928M10 2004M06
Included observations: 907

Autocorrelation	Partial Correlation		AC	PAC	Q-Stat	Prob
		1	-0.504	-0.504	230.92	0.000
		2	0.001	-0.338	230.92	0.000
		3	0.008	-0.244	230.99	0.000
		4	-0.043	-0.255	232.66	0.000
		5	0.058	-0.171	235.77	0.000
		6	-0.076	-0.241	240.99	0.000
		7	0.102	-0.122	250.53	0.000
		8	-0.078	-0.168	256.10	0.000
		9	0.057	-0.095	259.09	0.000
		10	-0.012	-0.063	259.23	0.000
		11	-0.087	-0.185	266.25	0.000
		12	0.137	-0.058	283.61	0.000
		13	-0.063	-0.030	287.28	0.000
		14	0.038	0.045	288.62	0.000
		15	-0.139	-0.149	306.37	0.000
		16	0.121	-0.092	320.01	0.000
		17	-0.050	-0.165	322.36	0.000
		18	0.090	-0.003	329.92	0.000
		19	-0.048	-0.013	332.04	0.000
		20	-0.035	-0.013	333.16	0.000
		21	0.020	-0.051	333.54	0.000
		22	0.009	0.018	333.62	0.000
		23	-0.047	-0.066	335.70	0.000
		24	0.043	-0.035	337.39	0.000
		25	0.052	0.057	339.91	0.000
		26	-0.100	-0.055	349.29	0.000
		27	0.089	0.082	356.67	0.000
		28	-0.049	0.064	358.95	0.000
		29	-0.031	0.025	359.83	0.000
		30	0.002	-0.120	359.83	0.000
		31	0.082	0.015	366.09	0.000
		32	0.001	0.095	366.09	0.000
		33	-0.101	0.066	375.73	0.000
		34	0.030	-0.063	376.61	0.000
		35	0.031	-0.012	377.51	0.000
		36	-0.042	-0.107	379.15	0.000

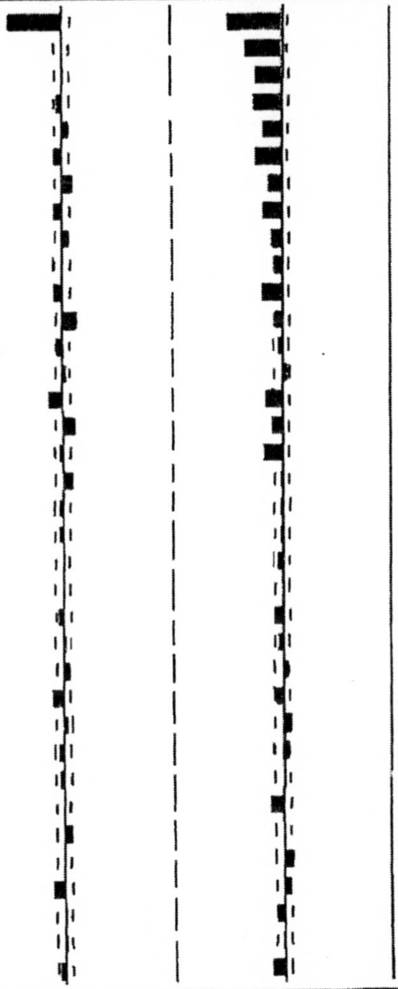

Figure 3.13: Correlogram of DJIA Monthly Close January 1930 to June 2004 (First Difference)

Date: 05/13/05 Time: 08:59
Sample: 1928M10 2004M06
Included observations: 908

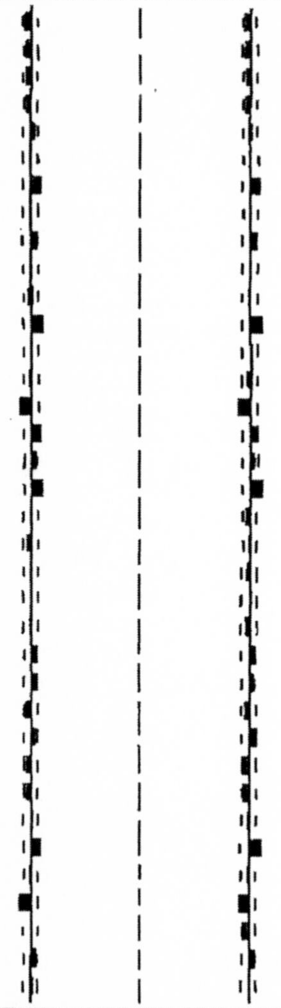

	AC	PAC	Q-Stat	Prob
1	-0.050	-0.050	2.3178	0.128
2	-0.041	-0.043	3.8329	0.147
3	-0.033	-0.038	4.8276	0.185
4	-0.042	-0.048	6.4316	0.169
5	0.036	0.028	7.5936	0.180
6	-0.009	-0.010	7.6613	0.264
7	0.099	0.098	16.607	0.020
8	-0.001	0.010	16.607	0.034
9	0.056	0.071	19.650	0.020
10	0.003	0.016	19.659	0.033
11	-0.029	-0.013	20.429	0.040
12	0.122	0.121	34.091	0.001
13	-0.015	0.003	34.285	0.001
14	-0.021	-0.024	34.690	0.002
15	-0.108	-0.110	45.562	0.000
16	0.099	0.087	54.661	0.000
17	0.055	0.042	57.431	0.000
18	0.117	0.130	70.198	0.000
19	-0.007	-0.017	70.239	0.000
20	-0.042	-0.012	71.855	0.000
21	-0.007	-0.018	71.904	0.000
22	0.005	0.032	71.927	0.000
23	-0.013	-0.031	72.091	0.000
24	0.072	0.062	76.967	0.000
25	0.070	0.045	81.571	0.000
26	-0.048	-0.046	83.725	0.000
27	0.049	0.075	85.955	0.000
28	-0.049	-0.064	88.204	0.000
29	-0.042	-0.052	89.862	0.000
30	0.032	-0.015	90.837	0.000
31	0.100	0.129	100.25	0.000
32	-0.010	-0.011	100.34	0.000
33	-0.116	-0.095	113.11	0.000
34	0.004	-0.064	113.12	0.000
35	0.055	0.065	115.94	0.000
36	0.034	0.014	117.04	0.000

coefficient seem to be alternating in a fairly regular pattern which is also a symptom of overdifferencing (Figure 3.12).

It is not unusual for overdifferenced data to be given more AR or MA terms to obtain better estimates. An immediate inclination by looking at PACF of the correlogram of Figure 3.12 would encourage the modeler to add more AR terms, because the PACF tells how many of such terms are likely to be needed. This does not necessarily improve the ability to have a stationary model or a superior forecast. In a similar manner one might be tempted to add MA terms; at least for the first lag as evidenced by the negative autocorrelation of the overdifferenced series because an MA term can partially cancel out a redundant order of differencing when the MA(1) coefficient is 1. These measures are not always successful. Differencing the data once suffices for this analysis to obtain a stationary model for forecasting.

The correlogram of Figure 3.11 typifies a random walk with a constant average trend. This makes it a prime candidate for single differencing resulting in a series with a mean reverting tendency. The constant term in the forecasting model is also representative of the *average trend-in-the trend;* where two or multiple differencing does not imply trends-in-trends. [32]

The elimination of the nonstationary trend by single differencing makes it unnecessary to add unnecessary AR terms to get rid of significant PACF coefficients. The first nonseasonal differencing of the series (Figure 3.13) illustrates that the series is reasonably stationary with very few significant autocorrelation coefficients. The solid line represents the zero axis; observations to the right of the line are positive values and those to the left are negative values. This correlogram exemplifies stationary series or a purely white noise process in which the autocorrelations hover around zero.

A closer look at Figure 3.13 indicates that an ARMA model may be a necessary forecasting model to get rid of the remaining autocorrelation coefficients. The series (stationarized) does not show an apparent AR or MA signature; where an MA signature could imply more MA terms and an AR signature, more AR terms. These signatures are normally associated with underdifferenced series and a positive autocorrelation at lag 1.

Modeling the series is a combination of what Salzman considers to be an art and science. ARIMA models are not necessarily models for which there are precise general rules after computation of data. There are, however, leading indicators in Econometric literature to assist the modeler with the modeling process.

Some of the prominent examples are related to the behavior of the ACF and PACF. For example, if the simple autocorrelations show seasonality (significant spikes after every twelve lags in a monthly data, the nonstationary series must be differenced with a gap approximating the seasonal variation before modeling.[33] Other examples include diagnosis for wave-like patterns of autocorrelations (which must be differenced and modeled with an autoregressive process); and the simultaneous convergence of partial and simple autocorrelation coefficient for successively longer lags (in which case the model may reflect an ARIMA process).

The model selected for the DJIA data incorporates the behavior of the correlogram after differencing the data and the response of the residuals to the model specification. The results of the model specification are reported in Table3.8 and the structure of the ARMA roots are reported in Table 3.9.The model which is the result of innumerable experiments, as should be expected with ARMA models, performs reasonably well with a very tight fit. All of the ARMA coefficients, as indicated by the t-statistic are significant (Table 3.8); the roots are stationary (they lie within the unit circle, or alternatively are not greater than 1); and the model is invertible (Table 3.9). The forecast for the adjusted model is provided in Figure 3.15.

The forecast, as evaluated by the variance proportion; the bias proportion; the Theil Inequality Coefficient (TIC); the root mean squared error (RMSE); and the correlogram of the residuals; turns out to be reasonably good (Figure3.15). The variance proportion is 0.003397; the bias proportion is 0.004396; the TIC is 0.004022; RMSE is 0.053977; and the correlogram of the residuals is provided in Figure 3.14.

The bias proportion indicates how far the mean of the forecast is from the mean of the actual series; the variance proportion indicates how far the variation is from the variation of the actual series; and the covariance proportion measures the remaining unsystematic forecasting error. It could be recalled that the RMSE is the weighted average error in the forecast and the Theil/TIC scales the error between 0 and 1; where 0 is a perfect fit and 1 is distant.

The correlogram of the residuals in Figure 3.14 achieves a white noise, which is the result of correct specification and no serial correlation in the residuals. It is evidently ocular that there are no significant spikes in the AR or PACF coefficients.

The conditions which are useful for evaluating the stability of the model (which is a difference equation) are provided in Table 3.9. The size/modulus of the complex roots/eigenvalues/parameters to be estimated must be less than one for the system to be stable. If the moduli of the eigenvalues are less than one, then the parameters to be estimated are within the unit circle; so that the model to be estimated could be written in inverted form if consideration is given to bounded sequences. Therefore the requirements for stability also imply model invertibility (MA roots must also be less than 1).[34] Eviews also gives the cycle corresponding to the imaginary roots (which are in conjugate pairs); for example (a+ bi) + (a-bi). The cycle is computed as $2\pi/a$; where a = a ratio of the imaginary and real parts of the root.

The model which is used to estimate the adjusted sample is then extended to the full sample before forecasting the monthly close of the DJIA in September of 2005. The results of the complete sample forecast are provided in Table 3.10 and the ARMA structure of the roots in Table 3.11. In both situations the results approximate that of the adjusted sample closely. The results of the forecast of the complete sample and the out of sample forecasts are provided in Figures 3.16 and 3.17. The forecast criteria—bias proportion; variance proportion; RMSE; and TIC are equally significantly positive.

Table 3.8: Result of ARIMA (9,1,5) for Adjusted Sample

Dependent Variable: LOG(CLOSE)
Method: Least Squares
Date: 05/15/05 Time: 15:09
Sample (adjusted): 1929M07 2004M06
Included observations: 900 after adjustments
Failure to improve SSR after 9 iterations
Backcast: 1929M02 1929M06

Variable	Coefficient	Std. Error	t-Statistic	Prob.
C	8.132577	13.30140	0.611408	0.5411
AR(4)	0.294288	0.082194	3.580404	0.0004
AR(6)	0.665034	0.077816	8.546202	0.0000
AR(9)	0.039561	0.018021	2.195217	0.0284
MA(1)	1.053192	0.026709	39.43192	0.0000
MA(2)	1.043425	0.039320	26.53646	0.0000
MA(3)	0.943957	0.041789	22.58873	0.0000
MA(4)	0.639646	0.077937	8.207170	0.0000
MA(5)	0.679234	0.077598	8.753222	0.0000
R-squared	0.998422	Mean dependent var		6.573333
Adjusted R-squared	0.998408	S.D. dependent var		1.359468
S.E. of regression	0.054249	Akaike info criterion		-2.980533
Sum squared resid	2.622125	Schwarz criterion		-2.932509
Log likelihood	1350.240	F-statistic		70460.53
Durbin-Watson stat	1.931930	Prob(F-statistic)		0.000000

Inverted AR Roots	1.00	.39+.80i	.39-.80i	.20-.34i
	.20+.34i	-.38	-.42+.82i	-.42-.82i
	-.98			
Inverted MA Roots	.39-.79i	.39+.79i	-.42+.84i	-.42-.84i
	-1.00			

Table 3.9: Structure of ARMA (9,1,5) Roots for Adjusted Sample

Inverse Roots of AR/MA Polynomial(s)
Specification: LOG(CLOSE) C AR(4) AR(6) AR(9)
MA(1) MA(2) MA(3) MA(4) MA(5)
Date: 05/15/05 Time: 15:15
Sample: 1928M10 2004M06
Included observations: 900

AR Root(s)	Modulus	Cycle
0.999798	0.999798	
-0.984145	0.984145	
-0.415411 ± 0.819143i	0.918456	3.079795
0.394157 ± 0.801307i	0.893003	5.641947
0.204849 ± 0.337867i	0.395116	6.125415
-0.382843	0.382843	

No root lies outside the unit circle.
ARMA model is stationary.

MA Root(s)	Modulus	Cycle
-0.997481	0.997481	
-0.422214 ± 0.837994i	0.938348	3.083757
0.394358 ± 0.786035i	0.879414	5.682101

No root lies outside the unit circle.
ARMA model is invertible.

Figure 3.14: Correlogram of Residuals for DJIA ARMA (9,1,5)

Date: 05/15/05 Time: 16:39
Sample: 1929M07 2004M06
Included observations: 900
Q-statistic probabilities adjusted for 8 ARMA term(s)

Autocorrelation	Partial Correlation		AC	PAC	Q-Stat	Prob
		1	0.030	0.030	0.7945	
		2	0.005	0.005	0.8216	
		3	0.029	0.029	1.5913	
		4	0.042	0.041	3.2190	
		5	0.053	0.051	5.7791	
		6	0.007	0.003	5.8187	
		7	0.039	0.037	7.2265	
		8	0.041	0.035	8.7831	
		9	0.089	0.083	15.921	0.000
		10	0.008	-0.001	15.982	0.000
		11	-0.015	-0.020	16.179	0.001
		12	0.039	0.029	17.540	0.002
		13	-0.009	-0.021	17.608	0.003
		14	-0.055	-0.065	20.421	0.002
		15	0.043	0.043	22.116	0.002
		16	-0.058	-0.070	25.248	0.001
		17	0.055	0.054	28.059	0.001
		18	0.066	0.062	32.086	0.000
		19	-0.015	-0.015	32.295	0.001
		20	-0.078	-0.080	37.939	0.000
		21	-0.056	-0.054	40.796	0.000
		22	0.046	0.045	42.784	0.000
		23	-0.023	-0.014	43.282	0.000
		24	0.028	0.032	44.017	0.000
		25	-0.017	-0.008	44.274	0.000
		26	0.032	0.030	45.240	0.000
		27	0.021	0.004	45.631	0.001
		28	-0.008	0.007	45.696	0.001
		29	0.019	0.032	46.036	0.001
		30	0.019	0.011	46.387	0.002
		31	0.017	0.017	46.647	0.002
		32	-0.010	-0.009	46.735	0.004
		33	-0.026	-0.034	47.366	0.004
		34	-0.031	-0.047	48.291	0.005
		35	-0.000	-0.012	48.291	0.007
		36	0.038	0.032	49.650	0.007

Table 3.10 Result of ARIMA (9,1,5) for Complete Sample

Dependent Variable: LOG(CLOSE)
Method: Least Squares
Date: 05/16/05 Time: 14:32
Sample (adjusted): 1929M07 2005M05
Included observations: 911 after adjustments
Failure to improve SSR after 17 iterations
Backcast: 1929M02 1929M06

Variable	Coefficient	Std. Error	t-Statistic	Prob.
C	8.326497	11.47510	0.725614	0.4683
AR(4)	0.299287	0.083522	3.583335	0.0004
AR(6)	0.659459	0.079691	8.275184	0.0000
AR(9)	0.039912	0.016591	2.405688	0.0163
MA(1)	1.052202	0.026668	39.45495	0.0000
MA(2)	1.041638	0.039174	26.58975	0.0000
MA(3)	0.943485	0.041250	22.87243	0.0000
MA(4)	0.633202	0.079859	7.928979	0.0000
MA(5)	0.672496	0.079646	8.443523	0.0000

R-squared	0.998488	Mean dependent var	6.605594
Adjusted R-squared	0.998474	S.D. dependent var	1.382414
S.E. of regression	0.053997	Akaike info criterion	-2.989939
Sum squared resid	2.629960	Schwarz criterion	-2.942375
Log likelihood	1370.917	F-statistic	74443.67
Durbin-Watson stat	1.932056	Prob(F-statistic)	0.000000

Inverted AR Roots	1.00	.39+.80i	.39-.80i	.21-.34i
	.21+.34i	-.38	-.41-.82i	-.41+.82i
	-.98			
Inverted MA Roots	.39-.78i	.39+.78i	-.42+.84i	-.42-.84i
	-1.00			

Table 3.11: Structure of ARMA (9,1,5) Roots for Complete Sample

Inverse Roots of AR/MA Polynomial(s)
Specification: LOG(CLOSE) C AR(4) AR(6) AR(9)
MA(1) MA(2) MA(3) MA(4) MA(5)
Date: 05/16/05 Time: 14:45
Sample: 1928M10 2005M05
Included observations: 911

AR Root(s)	Modulus	Cycle
0.999757	0.999757	
-0.983916	0.983916	
-0.413701 ± 0.818201i	0.916844	3.081606
0.391760 ± 0.800104i	0.890866	5.632749
0.206417 ± 0.339774i	0.397561	6.130698
-0.384791	0.384791	

No root lies outside the unit circle.
ARMA model is stationary.

MA Root(s)	Modulus	Cycle
-0.997486	0.997486	
-0.419663 ± 0.836488i	0.935857	3.086346
0.392305 ± 0.784775i	0.877368	5.674676

No root lies outside the unit circle.
ARMA model is invertible.

Figure 3.14: Forecast of Adjusted sample DJIA ARIMA (9,1,5)

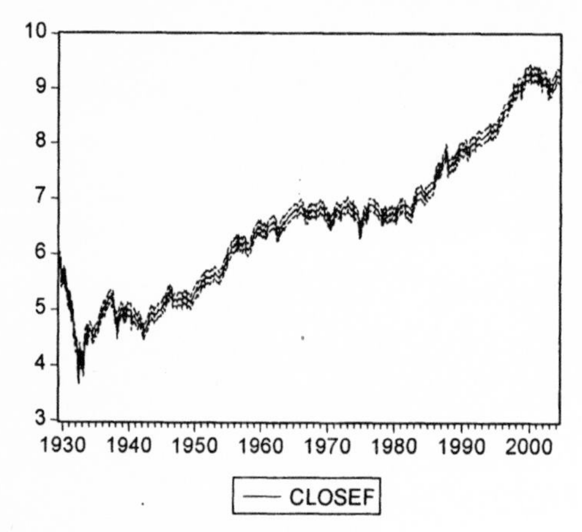

Forecast: CLOSEF
Actual: LOG(CLOSE)
Forecast sample: 1928M10 2004M06
Adjusted sample: 1929M07 2004M06
Included observations: 900

Root Mean Squared Error	0.053977
Mean Absolute Error	0.037630
Mean Abs. Percent Error	0.625925
Theil Inequality Coefficient	0.004022
Bias Proportion	0.004396
Variance Proportion	0.003397
Covariance Proportion	0.992208

Figure 3.15 Forecast of Complete Sample from the Adjusted Sample

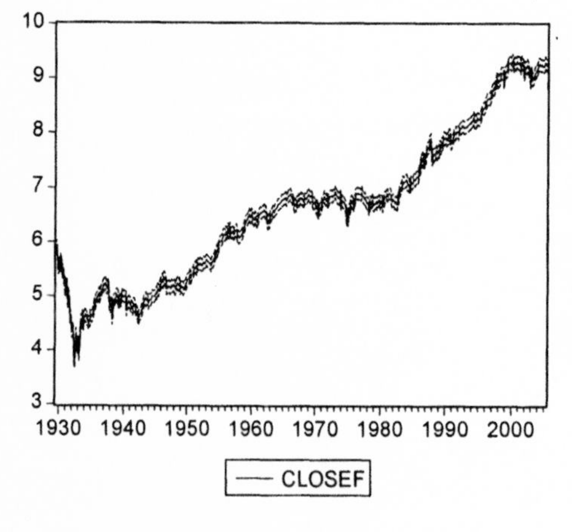

Forecast: CLOSEF
Actual: LOG(CLOSE)
Forecast sample: 1928M10 2005M05
Adjusted sample: 1929M07 2005M05
Included observations: 911

Root Mean Squared Error	0.053730
Mean Absolute Error	0.037467
Mean Abs. Percent Error	0.621396
Theil Inequality Coefficient	0.003982
Bias Proportion	0.004050
Variance Proportion	0.003156
Covariance Proportion	0.992795

Figure 3.17 Out-of-Sample (September, 2005) Forecast of DJIA

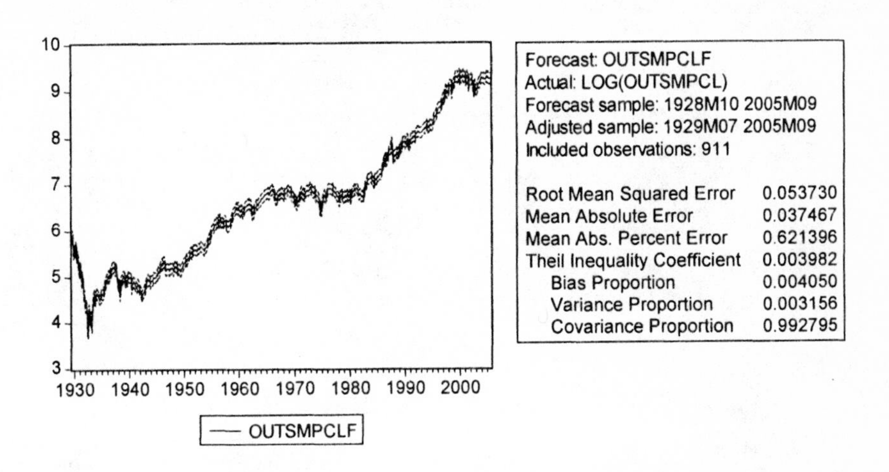

Forecasting has evident challenges but it has provided a method for individuals and businesses to make reasonable projections to minimize cost or maximize profit. In fact, it could reasonably be argued that it has provided a scientific method to make intelligent guesses rather than guessing in the dark.

The available forecasting options are diverse, but obviously they should be used with some precaution. Economic variables are usually interdependent and structural changes are less predictable than one might expect. Forecasting is therefore meaningful for short-term planning within the framework of reasonable assumptions. When the assumptions are rational and fortuitously gratifying forecasting becomes an enviable scientific guide; when the assumptions go sour the science is less enviable, but indispensable. The tendency for rational humans to plan ahead makes forecasting an inevitable method that would complement management science into the distant future.

Fortunately the methodology of forecasting has been evolving and will continue to do so. The next chapter deals with the optimization problems which are ever so often encountered by individuals and businesses dealing with competing uses of resources to minimize cost or maximize profit.

Exercises on Forecasting

1. (a) Collect a-twenty-year data on any financial or economic variable of your choice.
(b) Using Excel, Eviews, or any other software of your choice, plot the graph of the data you have collected.
(c) Explain whether or not your graph shows a trend or seasonality.
(d) Discuss the potential causes of the trend and seasonality if applicable.
(e) Use Excel to transform your data into a-four-year moving average. Graph the results of your four-year moving average. Compare and contrast the graph of your four-year moving average to your original graph.

2. Do a-one-year-ahead univariate forecast with data obtained for question 1(a). You must make sure you evaluate your model by first forecasting available data. Compare your result with professional estimates. Use the transformed data of 1(e) to do a univariate moving average forecast. Compare your result with professional estimates.

3. (a) How does financial and/or economic theory explain changes of the variable you have been working with? What variable could significantly affect the variable you have been working with? Why?
(b) Use a variable that could have significant impact on your prior model to construct a bivariate regression model of 30 observations and then do a bivariate forecast.
(c) Evaluate the results of your bivariate forecast against that of the univariate. How effective and efficient is your forecast (you may use the MSE; Theil; variance proportion; bias proportion; F-statistic; and/or R-squared/adjusted R-squared results)?

4. (a) Do you think an additional variable could improve your forecast? Assuming an additional variable could improve your forecast, construct a multivariate model of 30 observations and forecast your dependent variable. How does the multivariate result compare with the bivariate or univariate?
(b) Assuming you are the sales manager of a company, call it *Profit and Loss Ltd.*, what recommendations will you make to management in the next meeting for reducing cost or increasing profit?

5. With 50-100 observations or more, use the Box-Jenkins methodology to do a univariate forecast of your original variable. You may use the following steps: (i) check to see if the data is nonstationary and showing seasonality and/or a trend; (ii) difference the data appropriately if necessary; (iii) adjust your sample to evaluate your forecast; (iv) construct an AR, MA, or ARIMA model; (v) forecast the excluded portion of your data; and (vi) extend your data to do an out of sample forecast.

CHAPTER 4

CONSTRAINED OPTIMIZATION AND LINEAR PROGRAMMING

A universal problem facing individuals, corporate managers and policy makers is that of managing limited resources. Individuals make decisions about their spending habits based on choices and income limitations. Managers make decisions about the use of inputs (factors of production) to minimize cost and maximize profits. Policy makers make decisions about how to allocate resources to satisfy competing demands; in short to balance marginal social cost against marginal social benefits. In one form or another optimizing agents/subjects are faced with some sort of limitation which is largely related to the economizing problem of scarcity. It is therefore crucial for all agents to be able to obtain maximum satisfaction or outcome given some kind of constraint. The objective of obtaining the maximum satisfaction or result over time is the focus of dynamic optimization. When optimization is sought against a given constraint, optimization is generally considered to be constrained. The common denominator of all optimization problems, however, is obtaining what is best. In Economic literature this is perceived of as the quest for the best.

The economizing problem necessitates choices. The choices to be made may be legion or very limited. In all cases however, the choices to be made could be either very costly when wise decisions are not made or rewarding when prudent and wise decisions are made.

The most common criterion for making choices in Finance and Economics is to maximize profit, utility or growth which implicitly means the minimization of loss, disutility, or rate of decay. The nature of optimization problems necessitates a bifurcated specification. The first segment of the specification is considered the "objective function." Objective is synonymous with the goal or ambition. This goal is normally representative of the dependent variable discussed earlier in the regression models. The second segment of the specification is known as the "constraint."

The constraint defines the limitation of the objective function and is made up of choice variables which are otherwise known as decision or policy variables. These choice variables are the corollary of the independent variables in our prior regression models. In the dynamic optimization problems the goal is to obtain the best combination of the choice variables that will satisfy the required maximization or minimization (the combination of which is collectively referred to as *extremum* in Mathematics) of the objective function.

Optimization problems can be solved by: (i) simple partial derivatives; (ii) constrained optimization with single inequality constraint using the Lagrange function and partial derivatives; (iii) graphing for multiple constraints; and (iv) linear programming using the simplex algorithm to deal also with multiple constraints; where algorithm may be defined as "a set of rules or a systematic procedure for finding the solution to a problem."[35]

Multivariate Optimization

Multivariate optimization without constraint involves the determination of a maximum or minimum point of a function with more than two variables. Because it might be important to determine the effect on profit of a handbag or Toyota sold, or the effect on cost when an additional worker is hired or when a new computer is bought, the use of the partial derivative is instrumental in solving multivariable functions.

Consider the following example. Suppose the total profit function (π) of an American firm, *Profit and Loss Ltd*, is dependent on the sale of two goods—cases of Colgate (col) and bags of sugar (sug). Assume further that the profit function of *Profit and Loss Ltd* could be written as such:

$$\pi = f(\text{Col}, \text{sug}) = 60\text{Col} - 2\text{Col}^2 - 1\text{Col}*1\text{sug} - 4\text{sug}^2 + 200\text{sug}. \qquad (4.1)$$

How many cases of Colgate and bags of sugar should the firm sell to maximize profit? Since the profit function depends on the sale of Colgate and sugar, the function should be differentiated with respect to Colgate and sugar. When the partial derivative of the profit function is taken with respect to Colgate the marginal/incremental/additional effect of the sale of sugar on profit is assumed to be constant (i.e.) not changing. This enables us to see only the effect of an incremental change in the sale of Colgate on profit. Similarly when the partial derivative of the profit function is taken with respect to sugar the incremental effect of the sale of Colgate on the profit of *Profit and Loss Ltd* is assumed to be constant in order to isolate the marginal effect of the sale of sugar on profit. Differentiating the profit function with respect to Colgate gives:

$$\partial\pi/\partial col = 60 - 4col - 1sug = 0. \quad (4.2)$$

To solve for the optimal value of the independent variables the partial derivatives must be set equal to zero. By so doing each equation is set equal to the other which makes it feasible to solve for unknown values of the independent variable. It should be pointed out that the essence of the problem is not to determine extremum which requires a second derivative.[36] The partial derivative of the profit function with respect to sugar could be given as follows:

$$\partial\pi/\partial sug = 200 - 1col - 8sug = 0. \quad (4.3)$$

Multiplying equation 4.2 by -8 in order to solve the problem simultaneously for the unknown quantities gives the following result:

$$\begin{array}{l} -480 + 32col + 8sug = 0 \\ \underline{200 \ - \ 1col \ - 8sug = 0} \\ -280 + 31col \qquad = 0. \end{array} \quad (4.4)$$

Equation 4.4 is an easier representation of the challenge. It is now very easy to solve for the cases of Colgate that *Profit and Loss Ltd* would need to maximize profit. It would need to sell 9 cases of Colgate (i.e.) 280/31. Substituting the Colgate maximizing quantity into 4.2 or 4.3 will indicate the amount of sugar required for *Profit and Loss Ltd* to maximize profit. By substituting the quantity of Colgate into 4.2, the problem could be restated in the following form:

$$60 - 4(9) - 1sug = 0. \quad (4.5)$$

Equation 4.5 shows that *Profit and Loss Ltd* must sell 24 bags of sugar in order to maximize profit (i.e.) 60-36. Knowing the precise number of cases of Colgate and bags of sugar required to maximize profit for *Profit and Loss Ltd* also enables us to determine the maximum profit that *Profit and Loss Ltd* could make by plugging the profit maximizing quantities of Colgate and Sugar into the profit maximizing function of the firm (equation 4.1). The firm would make a maximum profit of $2142.

$$\pi = 60(9) - 2(9)^2 - 1(9)*1(24) - 4(24)^2 + 200(24) = \$2622.$$

Most problems confronting businesses have to deal with constraints which require them to make optimal choices. The optimization method selected would therefore depend on the type of constraint a business is confronted with. Assuming that *Profit and Loss Ltd* is confronted with a single constraint the *Lagrangian multiplier* could be a sufficient tool to solve the optimization problem. Functions for which the constraints are single and simple could also be solved by substitution.

Lagrangian Optimization

Maximizing profit or minimizing loss for a given constraint is not always easily obtained by the simple method of substitution. Therefore in much more complex cases using alternative methods may be necessary to solve for decision variables by using an explicit functional form. One of these alternative methods is popularly known as the *Lagrangian function*.

The *Lagrangian function* can be constructed through three easy procedures outlined in Dowling's *Introduction to Mathematical Economics*: (i) setting the constraint equal to zero; (ii) multiplying the constraint *by the Lagrange multiplier* (*lambda*, λ); and (iii) adding the product of the constraint to the original function—essentially combining the objective function and the constraint as one function.[37]

The typical *Lagrangian function* therefore has two component parts; the objective function which is a function of variables, $f(x,y)$; and a constraint of the form $g(x,y)=k$, where k is a constant. Rewriting the constraint in keeping with the first proposition means that the constraint can take the alternative form: $k-g(x,y)=0$. The original form could then be written as:

$$F(x,y,\lambda) = f(x,y) + \lambda[k-g(x,y)] \tag{4.6}$$

Because the constraint is set equal to zero, the product, $\lambda[k-g(x,y)]$, is also equal to zero and the addition of the constraint to the objective function does not change the value of the objective function. The critical values of all the independent variables could then be taken, set equal to zero, and solved for simultaneously. By so doing the *Lagrangian function* can also be treated as an unconstrained optimization problem, and its solution will always be identical to the original constrained optimization problem.[38]

Consider the following constrained optimization problem. Suppose a US firm in the US, call it *Big and Fat Ltd* is interested in minimizing its loss by using the appropriate amount of labor and capital (lk) to produce two fitness products *Superslim* capsules (*sup*) *and Megagym* trampolines (*meg*). Imagine further that the cost of the amount of labor and capital required to minimize the loss is equal to \$14 thousand and that the loss minimizing and constrained functions are given respectively as follows:

$$L = 2sup^2 + 3sup*meg + 3meg^2 \tag{4.7}$$

$$S.t. \quad \$14 \text{ thousand} = sup_{lk} + meg_{lk}. \tag{4.8}$$

How could *Big and Fat Ltd* determine the cost of *Superslim* capsules (s) and *Megagym* trampolines (m) that would minimize its resource cost using the *Lagrangian* method?

The first step would require us to set the constraint equal to zero. In abbreviated form, the constraint can be written alternatively as:

$$14{,}000 - s - m = 0. \tag{4.9}$$

Combining the constraint with the objective function and using the constraint parameter λ, or *Lagrangian multiplier* gives the following *Lagrangian function*:

$$L = 2sup^2 + 3sup*meg + 3meg^2 + \lambda[14{,}000 - s - m] \text{ or}$$

$$L = 2s^2 + 3s*m + 3m^2 + \lambda[14{,}000 - s - m] \tag{4.10}$$

By taking the partial derivatives of the *Lagrangian function* (*L*) with respect to *Superslim* capsules (*s*), *Megagym* trampolines (*m*), and *lambda* (λ), setting them equal to zero, and solving simultaneously *Big and Fat Ltd* could not only determine its minimizing cost of *Superslim* capsules and *Megagym* trampolines, it could also determine the shadow price (marginal cost/benefit) associated with the production of incremental units of the products by taking a look at the *lambda* coefficient. Taking the first-order partials and setting them equal to zero gives the following:

$$\partial L/\partial s = 4s + 3m - \lambda = 0 \tag{4.11}$$

$$\partial L/\partial m = 3s + 6m - \lambda = 0 \tag{4.12}$$

$$\partial L/\partial \lambda = 14000 - s - m = 0 \tag{4.13}$$

The system of equations can be solved simultaneously by multiplying 4.12 by negative one and subtracting it from 4.11 to give

$$s - 3m = 0; \text{ or } s = 3m. \tag{4.14}$$

Knowing the cost of *Superslim* capsules in terms of *Megagym* trampolines is valuable information to solve the system of equations. We could now solve for the actual cost of *Superslim* capsules, *Megagym* trampolines, and the shadow price. By plugging 4.14 into the constraint (4.13), we could solve for the exact cost of *Megagym* trampolines required to minimize loss. Equation 4.13 could now be written as:

$$14000 - 3m - m = 0; \text{ or } 4m = 14000. \tag{4.15}$$

Dividing 14000 by 4 indicates that $3,500 should be allocated to *Megagym* trampolines. Subtracting $3,500 from 14,000 leaves us with $10,500; the amount that should be allocated to the production of *Superslim* capsules. With knowledge of the cost of both *Superslim* capsules and *Megagym* trampolines required to minimize loss, the shadow price, λ, could now be easily calculated by plugging the values of s ($10,500) and m ($3,500) into either equation 4.11 or 4.12. Plugging the quantities into 4.11 gives us:

$$\lambda = 4(10{,}500) + 3(3{,}500) = \$52{,}500 \tag{4.16}$$

The value of *lambda* is informative. Beyond its mathematical appearance, it suggests that if the constraint is increased by a $1000 (i.e.) from $14,000 to $15,000, the loss that would be associated with the objective function would increase by $52,500. On the other hand if the constraint is reduced by $1000, the loss would be reduced by $52,500. This relationship of *lambda* to the objective function is generally characterized as the shadow price in economic literature. Our *Lagrangian function* could now be written as:

$$L=2(10{,}500)^2 + 3(10{,}500)*(3{,}500) + 3(3{,}500)^2 + 52{,}500[14{,}000 - 10{,}500 - 3{,}500]$$
$$= \$367,500000.$$

The *Lagrangian function* is a useful tool for optimization problems dealing with a single constraint. For real life business problems which involve more than one constraint other methods are more desirable. An approach that is capable of handling several constraints at the same time is known as *linear programming*. This work will consider two approaches to dealing with multiple constraints—graphing and Excel.

Optimization by Graphing

Although graphing could be used to solve optimization problems involving several constraints, graphing could accommodate only two variables because the graphing approach is restricted to representation in a two-dimensional space. Excel is much more capable of dealing with multivariable problems.

Consider the following optimization problem. Suppose a cosmetic firm, call it *Pretty Fannie Ltd*, is producing two types of body lotion, *Tender Care* (t) and *Loving Care* (l). Each lotion requires an anti-oxidant agent, *L-ascorbic acid* (a); a regenerating agent, *retinol palmitate* (r); and an antiaging agent, *ubiquinone* (u). To separate the effects of the two lotions on the skins of their customers, the firm decides to differentiate the concentration of the agents in the two lotions.

The firm decides that the winning formula for profit maximization is that *Tender Care* (t) should have 3.5% of *L-ascorbic acid* (a); 2% of *retinol palmitate* (r); and 1.5% of the antiaging agent *ubiquinone* (u). *Loving Care* on the other hand should have 1% of *L-ascorbic acid* (a); 1.5 % of *retinol palmitate* (r); and 3.5% of the antiaging agent *ubiquinone*. The firm keeps a close eye on its wage bill so that the workers are time constrained The workers of *Pretty Fannie Ltd* are required to spend no more than 15 hours on the *L-ascorbic acid* (a) agent; no more than 10 hours on the regenerating agent *retinol palmitate* (r); and more than 20 hours on the antiaging agent, *ubiquinone*. All time constraints apply to the preparation of the two lotions. The firm hopes to maximize the following profit function for thousands of dollars:

$$\pi = 2\ \textit{Tender Care}\ (t) + 5\ \textit{Loving Care}\ (l). \qquad (4.17)$$

What is the optimal solution? The answer might seem to be 7 *Tender Loving Care* but the optimal solution requires identifying the best use of time to satisfy the objective/profit function. Graphing problems of this nature invariably require a table so that the information can be quickly ocular and comprehensive. The information can be arranged as such:

Table 4.1 Summary of Optimization Constraints and Objective

Constraints	Objective function
L-ascorbic acid (*a*) $= 3.5(t) + 1(l) \leq 15$	$\pi = 2(t) + 5(l)$
Retinol palmitate (r) $= 2(t) + 1.5(l) \leq 10$	
Ubiquinone (u) $= 1.5(t) + 3.5(l) \leq 20$	
Nonnegativity $= t, l \geq 0$	

Table 4.1 gives a clear tabulation of the information to be computed and analyzed. The first three inequalities are considered the *technical constraints* and the fourth is a *nonnegativity constraint* to exclude unwanted or negative values from the solution. *Tender Care* (t) and *Loving Care* (l) are the *decision* or *structural* variables.

To solve the optimization problem graphically, the constraints must be rewritten in a manner that will make them amenable to providing a solution. For example,

$$a = 3.5(t) = 15 - 1(l) \qquad (4.18)$$

$$r = 2(t) = 10 - 1.5(l) \qquad (4.19)$$

$$u = 1.5(t) = 20 - 3.5(l). \qquad (4.20)$$

In the simplified form 4.18-4.20 can be easily solved for the intercept value. For example for constraint a when l is zero $t = (15/3.5) = 4.3$. If the workers of *Pretty Fannie Ltd* don't spend any time preparing *L-ascorbic acid* for *Loving Care* lotion, they will spend about 4 hrs and 18 minutes *preparing L-ascorbic acid* for the *Tender Care* lotion. On the contrary, if they don't spend any time preparing *L-ascorbic acid* for *Tender Care* , they will use up the allotted time (15 hours) preparing *L-ascorbic acid* for the *Loving Care* lotion.

A similar analogy could be made for the regenerating agent *Retinol palmitate* (r) and the antiaging agent *Ubiquinone* (u). The three constraints are shown on the left of Figure 4.1 as a, r, and u. The intercepts for t are 4.3; 5; and 13.3 respectively; and for l, 15; 6.7; and 5.7 respectively.

Figure 4.1 Graphs of Optimization Constraints and Feasible Region

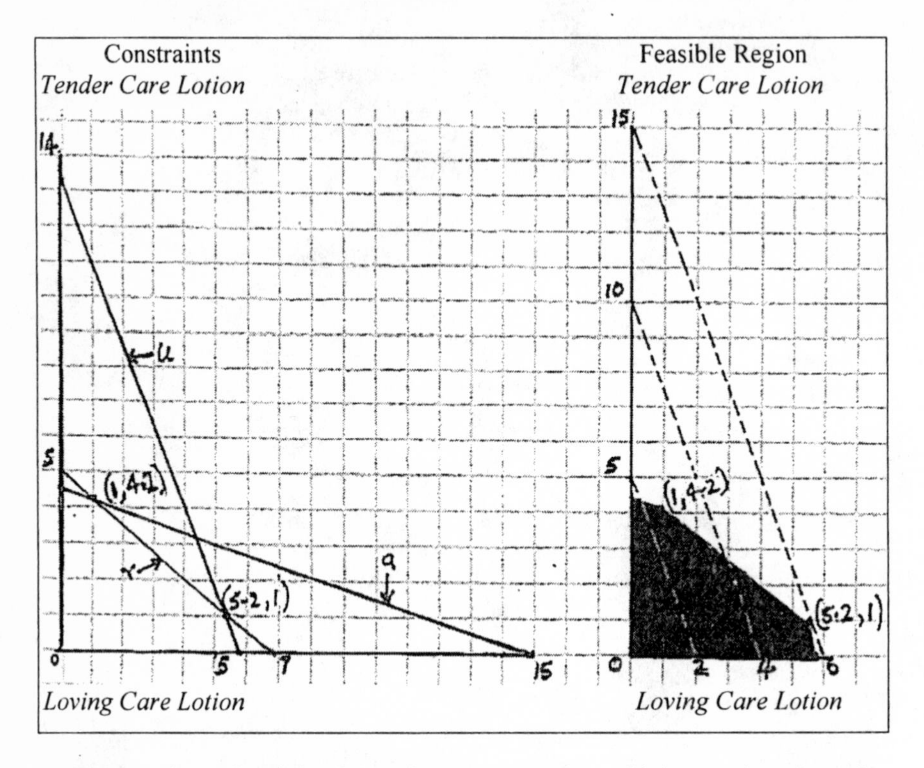

The graph on the right shows the extreme points which are taken from the graph on the left. These points are: 4.3; 1, 4.2; 5.2, 1; and 5.7. The extreme points define the feasible region (shaded area); the region which shows all the combinations for which the constraints (including the nonnegativity constraints) could be satisfied.

It is evident by now that the objective is to maximize profit. This means that the highest *isoprofit* line (6-15) on the graph on the right must be targeted for the greatest profit. This occurs at 5.2, 1.The slope of the *isoprofit* lines is calculated by solving the profit function (4.17) for t and taking the derivative with respect to l. Equation 4.21 summarizes the transformation:

$$t = \pi/2 - 5(l)/2 \quad \text{or} \quad \Delta t/\Delta l = -5/2. \qquad (4.21)$$

The slope is therefore -5/2. The solution obtained from the *isoprofit* lines makes it feasible to solve for the profit maximizing amount by plugging in the values of l and t. This translates into:

$$\pi = 2(1) + 5(5.2) = \$28 \text{ thousand.} \tag{4.22}$$

The graphing approach is helpful for dealing with multiple constraints but it should be recalled that it has the limitation of dealing with only two variables. It is also difficult to obtain precise coordinate values in decimal form. Analysis is largely dependent on best estimate and intuition. The approaches to optimization problems discussed so far are more academic as one would expect. Today the practical solution to optimization problems rely more on the use of technology. With the aid of modern technology, most contemporary businesses employ rapid techniques to deal with optimization issues which are less cumbersome. For example Excel and General Algebraic Modeling System (GAMS) have made optimization a lot faster and with comparatively less limitations. Optimization with Excel is discussed in the next section.

Optimization with Excel

One of the key advantages of excel is that it could accommodate multiple variables and multiple constraints. The entry procedures are simple, and with basic understanding of Excel, do not require extraordinary training. Excel could also easily accommodate quadratic specifications (i.e.) specifications which are not linear, or have exponents which are greater than one.

The key to using Excel for optimization problems is to make sure that *Solver* is installed and ready to go. Experience has shown that it is not always readily installed but that it could be installed by accessing the *Tools* menu option. By clicking on *Tools*, selecting *Add-Ins* from the drop down menu, and checking *Solver Add-in*, *Solver* could be installed and ready for use as an option in Excel under *Tools*.

As a simple introduction let us first consider the diet problem presented in Chiang's Fundamental *Methods of Mathematical Economics* and further analyzed within the linear programming framework by Ziggy MacDonald.[40] The problem is related to maintaining good health for which an individual must fulfill certain minimum daily requirements for certain types of nutrients.

For the sake of simplicity three kinds of nutrients are considered: (i) *calcium*; (ii) *protein*; and (iii) *vitamin A*. The decision or structural variables are only two foods (x_1 and x_2); which are considered as fish and milk here. The amount of fish and milk to be consumed is subject to price and minimum daily requirement limitations. Assume that the price of milk is 60 cents a tin and the price of fish is $1.00 per pound. The nutrients are to be consumed in units in order to easily permit round numbers in the example.

The minimum daily requirements of *calcium*, *protein,* and *vitamin A* from the consumption of fish and milk are 20, 20, and 12 units respectively. The hypothetical amounts of calcium, *protein,* and *vitamin A* to be obtained from each tin of milk are 10, 5, and 2 respectively; and for each pound of fish 4,5, and 6 respectively. What combination of fish and milk will satisfy the daily requirements at the least cost?

Once again a table would be in order before making entries into Excel. A table would make the task easier and comprehensive. It is probably apparent by now that the objective is to minimize cost whilst meeting the minimum daily requirements of the nutrients from the two foods. The objective is therefore to minimize a cost function based on prices and the limitations of constraints. The cost function to be minimized could be written as follows:

$$\text{Min. } c = \$0.6(\text{milk, } m) + \$1(\text{fish, } f); \tag{4.23}$$

$$\text{s.t.} \quad 10(m) + 4(f) \geq 20 \quad (\textit{calcium} \text{ requirement}) \tag{4.24}$$

$$5(m) + 5(f) \geq 20 \quad (\textit{protein} \text{ requirement}) \tag{4.25}$$

$$2(m) + 6(f) \geq 12 \quad (\textit{vitamin A} \text{ requirement}) \tag{4.26}$$

$$m, f \geq 0 \quad (\text{nonnegativity requirement}) \tag{4.27}$$

The nonnegativity condition precludes negative purchases. The weak inequality sign (≥) indicates that it is forbidden to fall below the daily requirements but okay to exceed the minimum amounts. Excel makes provision for this inequality without first adjusting for slacks. Equation 4.23 could be arranged in a table consistent with that of Chiang.

Table 4.2 Prices and nutrient contents of foods

	Milk (per tin)	Fish (per lb)	
Price	$0.60	$1.00	Minimum daily requirement
Calcium	10		20
Protein	5		20
Vitamin A	2		12

The information on the table can now be entered into Excel. There are no hard and fast rules as to which cell should be selected for what. It is important to note however that each cell must be used for a very specific or clear objective to avoid conflicts, inertia or spurious results. For the duration of our Excel discussion, data will be arranged vertically.

The cells in Excel are identified by columns and rows in a manner which is not very consistent with the way values of matrices are referenced. The rows are identified by Arabic numerals (1, 2, 3, 4...) and the columns by upper case English letters of the Alphabet (A, B, C...). References are first made to the Columns with the corresponding rows. This is important information for identifying variables and the values or mathematical expressions which are to be associated with variables. For example, if fish is entered in a cell, call it A6; this entry could be located by going to the first column (A) and the sixth row (6). If fish is to be multiplied by 2, using the formula bar and multiplying A6 by 2 (A6*2) will produce the required result. It may well be that a separate cell would be required for the result. Select the intended cell and in the formula bar enter the equal to sign (=) so that Excel would know that cell is being set aside for that value which is A6*2. In fact, the value in that cell, call it D3, could be made interactive with others.

The first challenge to solving the Chiang optimization problem in Excel is to identify cells in which the various categories of the problem and their corresponding values should be entered. This means setting aside separate cells for the decision variables, milk and fish; and separate cells for each and every constraint. Cells must also be selected for all values (including prices) associated with the variables and the constraints. For example the following information could be entered in the Excel spreadsheet as follows:

Table 4.3 Excel Entries of the Nutrition Optimization Problem[40]

	A	B	C	D	E
1				Prices	
2	Min.	=D2*B4+D3*B5		0.6	
3				1	
4	Milk				
5	Fish				
6					
7	St.				
8					
9	Calcium	=10*B4+4*B5	20		
10	Protein	=5*B4+5*B5	20		
11	Vita. A	=2*B4+6*B5	12		
12	Non-neg 1	=B4	0		
13	Non-neg 2	=B5	0		
14					

The objective function is defined in B2, and A2 reminds the user of the objective; which is to minimize cost or expenses on milk and fish. The details in B2 are an exact representation of the information on the right side of the 4.23 equality equation. D2 represents 60 cents (0.6); B4, the undecided amount of milk to be consumed; D3, the price of fish; and B5 the undecided amount of fish to be consumed. It could be quickly noticed that letter-number combinations could easily define interactive variables and objectives.

The constraints are defined in cells B9, B10, B11, B12, and B13; and they represent equations 4.24, 4.25, 4.26, and 4.27 respectively. For example, the constraint on *calcium* is given in cell B9; which is 10 times the unknown value of milk plus 4 times the unknown value of fish. It should be recalled that cells B4 and B5 represent these unknown values of milk and fish to be calculated by Excel *solver*. The non-negativity conditions apply to the decision variables, milk and fish; which cannot be negative. Allusion is made once again to the two cells representing milk and fish for the non-negativity requirement. It should be pointed out that separate cells are set aside for the requirement. Column *C* contains the minimum requirements which will play a greater role when the user gets into the Excel *Solver* option.

After the entries have been made clearly and correctly the user could then go to *Tools* on the Excel task bar and select *Solver* from the drop down menu. The *Solver Parameters* window would open up. It is very important to reference the entries correctly. The *Target Cell* is the cell to be minimized or maximized; the equivalent of B2 in our example. An easier way to reference cells in Excel is to click on the cells. Excel would automatically enter the cells. Alternatively the cells could be manually typed into the boxes and Excel would automatically record the $ sign.

Excel requires the user to indicate whether the objective is to maximize or minimize the *Target Cell*. The selection could be made by selecting Max or Min next to *Equal To* in the *Solver Parameters*. In order for *Solver* to provide a solution to the optimization problem it must be given information about the structural or decision variables. It could be recalled that these are defined as B4 and B5 (milk and fish) in our example. These cells must be entered in the *By Changing Cells* box. Alternatively Excel could guess, but it will be more prudent to do this virtual effortless work.

The constraint box is capable of holding multiple constraints and is entitled "*Subject to the Constraints*". To input the constraints click on *Add*. An *Add Constraint* window would open up which would require specification of *Cell Reference*, the equality or weak inequality requirement, and the constraint. It is very easy for the inequality sign to be forgotten or selected wrongly. The user must be very careful when selecting the equality or inequality sign and it is strongly suggested that the selection be reviewed at least twice. The downward arrow next to the equality or inequality sign allows the user to select his preference. The three most popular choices in optimization problems are: (i) equal to (=); (ii) less than or equal to (<=); and (iii) greater than or equal to (>=). The "greater than or equal to" sign barely sets the constraint as a minimum. It is therefore okay to exceed the constraint but not okay to fall below it. The "less than or equal to" sign sets a maximum. It is not okay to exceed the constraint.

In the *Cell Reference* box indicate the constraints appropriately one at a time. In our example the *Cell Reference* for the *calcium* constraint would be B9. Since the relevant inequality sign for this constraint is greater than or equal to it must be selected by using the down-arrow. The information in column *C* now becomes highly pertinent and these values must be entered in the box asking for the *Constraint*. In the case of *calcium* the cell holding the relevant constraint would be C9. Watching the equality or inequality sign for each constraint is important because for a single optimization problem there is no reason why the restrictions or limitations on the decision variables might not change from one constraint to another. It is also important to enter the non-negativity requirements as part of the constraints. Excel also makes provision to add, change or modify, and delete constraint(s).

Once the *Solver Parameters* have been entered, Excel would be ready to provide a solution to the optimization problem. By clicking on the solve button Excel would take the user to a *Solver Results* window. If a successful execution of the entries are made in *Solver* Excel would inform the user that "*Solver* found a solution" and that "[a]ll constraints and optimality conditions are satisfied." The user has the option of selecting one of three or all reports; namely: (i) answer; (ii) sensitivity; and (iii) limits.

It is important to make sure that the default *Keep Solver Solution* is checked for the acquisition and retention of prompt and final solutions to be recorded against the decision variables and the constraints. The Excel *Answer* and *Sensitivity Reports* are provided in Tables 4.4 and 4.5. The *Answer Report* provides the final value for the minimum cost ($2.8); the combined units of the nutrients for milk and fish (*calcium*, 34; *protein*, 20; and *vitamin A*, 12); the status (i.e.) whether the constraints are binding or nonbinding based on the optimality result; and the slack (excess or shortfall) using the constraint as a benchmark measure. The optimization results show that the constraints are binding on *protein* and *vitamin A* but not *calcium* which has a slack of 14 units in excess of the minimum. The *Answer Report* also gives the amount of milk (3) and fish (1) that could be consumed given the constraints.

The *Sensitivity Report* (Table 4.5) provides opportunity for post-optimality analysis. It shows the response of the objective function to incremental or marginal changes in the constraint parameters. It could be recalled that similar analysis was done earlier when the *Lagrangian Multiplier* (λ) was discussed. "Sensitivity" is a code for the measurement of responsiveness, elasticity, marginalism or the shadow price. For example, if the consumption of *vitamin A* should go up from 12 units to 13 units for both milk and fish, the cost of consuming milk and fish would increase by 9 cents (0.09). If on the other hand the consumption is decreased by 1 unit, the cost of consuming milk and fish would fall by 9 cents. Therefore the *Lagrange Multiplier* is an indicator of the shadow price.

The *Sensitivity Report* is also useful for evaluating the range of optimality or the maximum allowable increase: MacDonald shows that if an adjustment is made to the objective coefficients as long as the sum of the adjustment as expressed by the allowable increase/decrease does not exceed 100%, the value of the objective function would change but not the optimal values of the decision variables. The *Limits Report* provides no additional information and is not reported here.

There are certain important ideas which should be taken away from the nutrition example. First it is exceedingly crucial to identify the decision variables and their coefficients; second, the objective function of the optimization problem must be well understood because the objective function is the purpose of the optimization exercise and what must be referenced as the *Target Cell* in *Solver*; third, the user solves for the decisions variables by entering the prospective solution cells of these variables in the *By Changing Cells* box in *Solver*; fourth, the constraint inequalities or equalities must be properly entered; and finally, an understanding of the shadow price is very important to assess the responsiveness of the objective function to incremental constraint adjustments which is an integral component of post optimality analysis.

Table 4.4 Excel Optimization *Answer Report*

Microsoft Excel 10.0 Answer Report
Worksheet:[Book1]Sheet1
Report Created: 5/29/2005 6:29:38PM

Target Cell (Min)

Cell	Name	Original Value	Final Value
$B$2	min	0	2.8

Adjustable Cells

Cell	Name	Original Value	Final Value
$B$4	milk	0	3
$B$5	fish	0	1

Constraints

Cell	Name	Cell Value	Formula	Status	Slack
$B$9	calcium	34	$B$9>=$D$9	Not Binding	14
$B$10	protein	20	$B$10>=$D$10	Binding	0
$B$11	vita A	12	$B$11>=$D$11	Binding	0
$B$13	nonneg 2	1	$B$13>=$D$13	Not Binding	1
$B$12	nonneg 1	3	$B$12>=$D$12	Not Binding	3

Table 4.5 Excel Optimization *Sensitivity Report*

Microsoft Excel 10.0 Sensitivity Report
Worksheet: [Book1]Sheet1
Report Created: 5/29/2005 6:29:38PM

Adjustable Cells

Cell	Name	Final Value	Reduced Gradient
$B$4	milk	3	0
$B$5	fish	1	0

Constraints

Cell	Name	Final Value	Lagrange Multiplier
$B$9	calcium	34	0
$B$10	protein	20	0.080000007
$B$11	vita A	12	0.099999994
$B$13	non-neg 2	1	0
$B$12	non-neg 1	3	0

The purpose of optimization in this section is understandably to recognize the practical relevance and comparative flexibility of Excel. We would therefore now consider a-three-variable example. Consider a firm, *Thrifty West*, which is trying to minimize cost so that it could maximize profit. The firm has three branches: one in New York; another in Chicago; and the third in Nova Scotia.

The firm is exceedingly concerned about its cash outflows in the three cities. At the top of its expenses are utilities, wages and supplies. Suppliers of raw materials must be paid as well as wages and utility bills. The managers of *Thrifty West* are curious to know how best they could minimize cash outflows for a combination of utility, wage, and supplies cash outflows. They however want the total monthly usage of utilities, payment of wages, and purchases of supplies in New York to be greater than or equal to 40%; in Chicago, to be greater than or equal to 30%; and in Nova Scotia, to be greater than or equal to 10%. They are interested in minimizing the following cost function:

$$\text{Min. } C = 0.5\text{utilities (u)} + 0.2\text{wages (w)} + 0.3\text{ supplies(s)} \quad (4.28)$$

The cost function must be minimized subject to the following constraints:

$$\text{New York: } 0.1\text{ utilities (u)} + 0.2\text{ wages (w)} + 0.2\text{ supplies(s)} \geq 0.4 \quad (4.29)$$

Chicago: 0.2 utilities (u) + .02 wages (w) + 0.05 supplies(s) $\geq$ 0.3 (4.30)

Nova Scotia: 0.02 utilities (u) + 0.05 wages (w) + .1 supplies(s) $\geq$ 0.1 (4.31)

The *Thrifty West* optimization problem can also be illustrated in the following Excel format (Table 4.6):

Table 4.6: Maximizing Profit by Minimizing Cash Outflows

	A	B	C	D	E
1				Coefficients	
2	Min	=D2*B4+D3*B5+D4*B6		0.5	
3				0.2	
4	Utilities			0.3	
5	Wages				
6	Supplies				
7					
8					
9	s.t.				
10					
11	N. York	=.1*B4+.2*B5+.2*B6	0.4		
12	Chicago	=.2*B4+.02*B5+.05*B6	0.3		
13	N. Scotia	=.02*B4+.05*B5+.1*B6	0.1		
14	Non-neg 1	=B4	0		
15	Non-neg 2	=B5	0		
16	Non-neg 3	=B6	0		
17					

Apart from the additional variable count, Table 4.6 illustrates a standard entry procedure for the simple linear programming problem. The cells are appropriately referred to by their letters and numbers and for the sake of simplicity and consistency B2 remains the *Target Cell.*

The decision variables are utilities, wages and supplies, and their coefficients are respectively listed in column *D*. The constraints for the cash outflows on the cities (New York, Chicago, and Nova Scotia) are given in B11-B13. The non-negativity conditions (B4-B6) ensures that spending on the decision variables is not negative. By Accessing *Solver* in Excel using the methods outlined earlier on a solution will be provided to the optimization problem. The solutions are provided in Tables 4.7 and 4.8.

Table 4.7 *Answer Report* for Minimizing Cash Outflows

Microsoft Excel 10.0 Answer Report
Worksheet:[Book1]Sheet1
Report Created: 5/30/2005 10:09:09 PM

Target Cell (Min)

Cell	Name	Original Value	Final Value
$B$2	max	0.952331608	0.952331608

Adjustable Cells

Cell	Name	Original Value	Final Value
$B$4	utilities	1.347150261	1.347150261
$B$5	wages	1.191709838	1.191709838
$B$6	supplies	0.134715031	0.134715031

Constraints

Cell	Name	Cell Value	Formula	Status	Slack
$B$16	nonneg3	0.34715031	$B$16>=$C$16	Not Binding	0.134715031
$B$11	NY	0.4	$B$11>=$C$11	Binding	0
$B$12	Chicago	0.300000001	$B$12>=$C$12	Binding	0
$B$14	nonneg1	1.347150261	$B$14>=$C$14	Not Binding	1.347150261
$B$15	nonneg2	1.191709838	$B$15>=$C$15	Not Binding	1.191709838
$B$13	Nova Scotia	0.1	$B$13>=$C$13	Binding	0

Table 4.7 shows that the constraints on New York, Chicago, and Nova Scotia are binding. There are however slacks for utilities, wages, and supplies. The optimizing percentage of cash outflows for utilities, wages, and supplies in the three cities are 1.3, 1.2, and 0.13 respectively. Spending at this level would enable *Thrifty West* to minimize cost by 95 percent.

Of additional interest are the *Lagrange Multiplier* results in the *Sensitivity Report* of Table 4.8. It is probably apparent by now that they indicate shadow prices. Increasing the constraint in New York by 1% would lead to a 0.6 % increase in the cash outflow of the firm. Reducing the cost in Chicago by 1% would result in a 2% decrease in the cash outflow of the firm. A 1% increase/decrease in expenditures in Nova Scotia would lead to a 0.7% increase/decrease in the cash outflow of *Thrifty West*. This analysis could be extended to additional variables.

Excel could also be used for optimization problems with quadratic expressions. A typical quadratic optimization problem is one with a quadratic objective function of the decision variables and linear functions of the constraints. The objective function could therefore take the form: $2p^2 + 5t^2 + pt$. Exponents could be entered by using the upward arrow on keyboards (usually above the number

6). You may set a separate cell aside for exponents and then reference that cell. The reader will be given an opportunity to deal with the quadratic challenge in the optimization exercises at the end of this chapter.

Table 4.8 Minimizing Cash Outflows *Sensitivity Report*

Microsoft Excel 10.0 Sensitivity Report
Worksheet: [Book1]Sheet1
Report Created: 5/30/2005 10:09:10 PM

Adjustable Cells

Cell	Name	Final Value	Reduced Gradient
$B$4	utilities	1.347150261	0
$B$5	wages	1.191709838	0
$B$6	supplies	0.134715031	0

Constraints

Cell	Name	Final Value	Lagrange Multiplier
$B$16	nonneg3	0.134715031	0
$B$11	NY	0.4	0.606217593
$B$12	Chicago	0.300000001	2.124352295
$B$14	noneg1	1.347150261	0
$B$15	nonneg2	1.191709838	0
$B$13	NovaScotia	0.1	0.725388741

The objective of this book has been to simplify concepts which might otherwise be strange and convoluted to young researchers, students in Economics and business classes or even young professionals who need a quick insight into the key concepts of research, time series data estimation for forecasting, and constrained optimization. The concepts have been deliberately chosen because of their relevance to business courses and the everyday operations of businesses. Because of its cursory and didactic purpose, this text is intended to complement relevant texts in the areas of research and optimization. It is hoped that at the end of this chapter the reader has obtained a practical understanding of some of the basic quantitative challenges in the study of Finance, Economics, and to some extent, other social sciences.

Exercises on Constrained Optimization and Linear Programming

1. Suppose the total cost function of a firm is given as such:

$$TC = 5Q^2 + 2\,Q + 15;$$ where TC is total cost and Q is quantity.

Differentiate the TC function with respect to Q to get the marginal cost (MC) function. How would you interpret your result? Evaluate the MC function at 2.

2. Suppose the profit function of a firm selling two distinct products shoes (s) and bags (b) is:

$$\pi = 20(s) - 3(s)^2 - sb - 2b^2 + 75b.$$

What is the approximate profit maximizing quantity of shoes and bags that this firm should sell?

3. Use the *Lagrangian* method to optimize the following objective function

$$f(x,y) = 4x + 3y$$

subject to the following constraint: $x^2 + y^2 = 10$. What is the meaning of the *Lagrange Multiplier* in this case?

4. A firm, *Spend and Fear Not Ltd*, wants to maximize profit from the sale of two products, *Poka Jeans* (p) *and Teddy Bears* (t). The firm is interested in maximizing the profit function $\pi = 30p + 10t$, subject to the following constraints: (i) $4p + 2t \leq 40$; (ii) $2p + 4t \leq 10$; and $t \leq 7$. With the aid of graph papers, use the graphing method to solve for the optimal combination of *Poka Jeans* and *Teddy Bears* and the expected amount of profit?

5. A firm produces three products, radios; computers; and cellular phones by using three inputs, capital (k); labor (L); and *entrepreneurial* skill (e). The firm is very concerned about its resource cost and wants to minimize the cost of production. The objective function to be minimized is of the form

$$\text{min.} \quad c = 15k^2 + 10L^2 + e^2$$

subject to the following constraints: (i) cellular phones: $5k + 3L + 2e$; (ii) computers: $10k + 2L + 5e$; and radios; $3k + 2L + 2e$. Use an Excel spreadsheet and Excel *Solver* to solve the optimization problem and interpret the *Lagrange multiplier* results.

NOTES

1. See http://www.nyse.com
2. Engel, N and H. Hecht, *How to Buy Stocks*, pp. 73-74.
3. Year-to-date (YTD) turnover is computed by multiplying YTD average daily volume by the number of trading days in the current year and dividing by the average of total shares outstanding at the end of the previous year and the total shares outstanding at the end of the given month.
4. See http://www.federalreserve.gov/rnd.htm
5. Current base year is 1997.
6. See http://www.bls.gov/home.htm
7. The other bureaus were the Bureau of Naturalization, the Bureau of Immigration, and the Children's Bureau.
8. Revisions in the Industrial Price Program included constructing the Producer Price Index (PPI) on stage-of-processing analysis and transaction prices. The Employment Cost Index (ECI), which measures relative changes in total compensation (wages and salaries plus employee benefits), was extended to cover state and local government workers, and the farming and household sectors. In the sphere of occupational safety and health statistics more information was obtained from additional states which supplied information on injuries and illnesses based on workers' compensation records.
9. See http://www.bls.gov/news.release/cpi.nr0.htm
10. See http://www.bea.doc.gov/
11. See http://www.bea.doc.gov/bea/about/mission.htm
12. See Daniel H. Garnick, "Differential Regional Multiplier Models," Journal of Regional Science 10 (February 1970): 35-47; and Ronald L. Drake, "A Short-Cut to Estimates of Regional Input-Output Multipliers," International Regional Science Review 1 (Fall 1976): 1-17.
See also http://www.bea.doc.gov/ bea/ regional/rims/brfdesc.cfm
13. See http://www.census.gov/svsd/www/adseries.html
14. See http://www.census.gov/acsd/www/history.html
15. See Baumohl, B. *The Secrets of Economic Indicators*, p. 63.
16. See http://www.cbot.com/cbot/pub/page/0,3181,942,00.html
17. Ibid.
18. See http://www.nasdaq.com/
See http://finance.yahoo.com/ for user-friendly historical data on NASDAQ, DOW, S&P 500, 10-year bond, NYSE and NASDAQ volumes of trade quotes. Provision is also available for instant Excel query result.
19. See http://www.sca.isr.umich.edu/main.php
Also see Baumohl, B. *The Secrets of Economic Indicators*, pp. 91-92 for the construction of the index.
19. See http://www.worldbank.org
20. See http://web.worldbank.org/wbsite/external/reserach/extprospects/gdfex...
21. See http://www.IMF.org

22. See http://www.imf.org/external/np/exr/facts/globstab.htm
23. See http://ifs.apdi.net/imf/about.asp
24. See http://www.transparency.org
25. The margin of error associated with polls is given by $z*\sqrt{[p(1-p)/n]}$; where z is the z-score for a level of confidence (1.96 for a 95% confidence level); p is the ratio of respondents to the sample size; and n is the sample size.
26. The slope is given by $\Sigma(x_i*y_i)/\Sigma x_i^2$; where x_i is the deviation of each x_i observation from its mean and y_i is the deviation of each y_i observation form its mean. Alternatively it could be written as $r*(s_y/s_x)$; where r is the correlation coefficient and s_y and s_x is the standard deviation of y and x respectively. The predicted value of each y observation, normally written as y hat is just $a+bX$; where a is the intercept; b is the slope; and X the independent variable.
27. $F = [R^2/(k-1)]/(1-R^2)/(n-k)$; where k is the number of coefficients estimated and n is the number of observations.
28. Taylor's Rule = $FFR_r = 2 + 0.5(\pi-2) - 0.5(\text{GDP gap})$; where π = rate of inflation and GDP gap, the percentage deviation of real GDP (Y) from its natural rate (Y'), =100*(Y'-Y)/Y'. The Real Funds Rate (RFR_r) is the difference between the nominal FFR and the inflation rate.
29. A basis point is $1/100^{th}$ of one percent or 0.0001.
30. Maddala, G.S. and In-Moo Kim, *Unit Roots, Cointegration, and Structural Change*; p. 18. For a much fuller discussion of correlograms see Damodar Gujarati's *Basic Econometrics*, pp.842-846; and Jack Johnston and John DiNardo's, *Econometric Methods*, pp.217-241.
31. See http://www.duke.edu/~rnau/411arim2.htm
32. Ibid.
33. Seasonal accommodation for the DJIA data would mean generating a new work file in Eviews by choosing *Genr* in Eviews and setting the dependent variable equal to "lclose – lclose(-12)".
34. For a fuller and complete discussion, see James Hamilton's *Time Series Analysis*, pp. 30-36.
35. See Edward Dowling's *Introduction to Mathematical Economics*, p.331.
36. For extremum problems see Alpha Chiang's *Fundamental Methods of Mathematical Economics* p.233-253 and Dowling *op.cit.* pp 76-88.
37. Dowling, op. cit. p.105.
38. See Dominick Salvatore's *Managerial Economics in the Global Economy*, p. 62.
39. Ziggy MacDonald, "Teaching Linear Programming Using Microsoft Excel Solver" Cheer: Computers in Higher Education Economics Review, vol. 9 issue 3, 1995. See also Chiang's *Fundamental Methods of Mathematical Economics*, p. 652.
40. See Ziggy MacDonald, "Economic Optimisation: An Excel Alternative to Estelles et al's GAMS Approach" Cheer: Computers in Higher Education Economics Review, vol 10 issue 3, 1996.

Bibliography

Baumohl, Bernard. *The Secrets of Economic Indicators*, Pennsylvania: Wharton School Publishing, 2005.

Bowerman, Bruce and Richard O'Connell. *Forecasting and Time Series: An Applied Approach*, California: Duxbury, 1993.

Burton, Maureen and Lombra Ray. *The Financial System and The Economy*, US: Thomson South-Western, 2003.

Chiang, Alpha. *Fundamental Methods of Mathematical Economics*, New York: McGraw-Hill, 1984.

Chicago Board of Trade. 2005. *CBOT DataExchange*. Http://cbotdataexchange.if5.com/default.aspx. 20 March, 2005.

Chicago Board of Trade. 2005. *Futures Tutorial*. Http://www.cbot.com/cbot/docs/futures_tutorial.html. 20 March, 2005.

Chicago Board of Trade. 16 October, 2001. *Mission Statement*. Http://www.bls.gov/bls/blsmissn.htm.

Chicago Board of Trade 2005. *Our History*. Http://www.cbot.com/cbot/pub/page/0,3181,942,00.html.

Dowling, Edward. *Introduction to Mathematical Economics*, New York: McGraw- Hill, 1992.

Engel, Louis and Henry Hecht. *How to Buy Stocks*, Boston: Little Brown and Company, 1994.

Fabozzi, Frank, ed. *The Handbook of Financial instruments*, New Jersey: John Wiley and Sons, 2002.

Federal Reserve Board of Governors. 3 January, 2000. *Foreign Exchange Rates*. Http://www.federalreserve.gov/releases/g5a/20000103/G5A.htm.

Federal Reserve Board of Governors. 11 March, 2005 *Foreign Exchange Rates*. Http://www.federalreserve.gov/releases/h10/update/

Feiring, Bruce. *Linear Programming : An Introduction*, Newbury Park: Sage Publications, 1986.

Gilliland 2002. *Is Forecasting A Waste of Time? Problem Background* Http://www.keepmedia.com/jsp/article_detail_print.jsp. 27 February, 2005.

Griffiths, William, R. Carter Hill, and George Judge. *Learning and Practicing Econometrics*, New York: John Wiley and Sons, 1993.

Gujarati, Damodar. *Basic Econometrics*, Boston: McGraw Hill, 2003.

Hamilton, James. *Time Series Analysis*, New Jersey: Princeton University Press, 1994.

Harrison, Michael. 2004. *Understanding the Corruption Perceptions Index: Application Issues for The Foreign Direct Investment Decision.* Http://www.snhu.edu/img/assets/3655/Understanding_the_CPI _Application_Issues_in_the_FDI_Ivestment_Decision.doc. 10 April, 2005.

Hendry, David and Neil Ericsson, eds. *Understanding Economic Forecasts*, Cambridge: The MIT Press, 2003.

International Monetary Fund 2004. *About The IMF*. Http://www.Imf.org/ external/about.htm 28 March, 2005.

International Monetary Fund. 2005. *About The IFS Online Service*. Http://ifs.apdi.net/imf/about.asp. 3 April, 2005.

International Monetary Fund. 2005. *The IMF At a Glance*. Http://www.imf.org/ External/np/exr/facts/glance.htm. 3 April, 2005.

Johnston, Jack and John Dinardo. *Econometric Methods*, New York; McGraw-Hill, 1997.

Kidwell, David et.al. *Financial Institutions, Markets and Money*, New Jersey: John Wiley and Sons, 2003.

Krugman, Paul. 1993. *Exchange Rates*. Http://www.econlib.org/library/Enc/ ExchangeRates.html. 6 May, 2005.

Lind, Douglas, William Marchal and Samuel Wathen. *Statistical Techniques in Business and Economics*, Boston: McGraw- Hill, 2005.

Maddala, G. S. *Introduction to Econometrics*, Chichester: John Wiley and Sons, 2001.

Maddala, G. S. and In-Moo Kim. *Unit Roots, Cointegration and Structural Change*, Cambridge: Cambridge University Press, 2000.

MacDonald, Ziggy. "Economic Optimisation: An Excel Alternative to Estelles et al's GAMS Approach," *Computers in Higher Education Economics Review*, vol.10, no.3 (1996): 2-5.

MacDonald, Ziggy. "Teaching Linear Programming using Microsoft Excel Solver," *Computers in Higher Education Economics Review*, vol.9, no.3 (1995): 7-10.

Mankiw, Gregory. *Macroeconomics*, New York: Worth Publishers, 2003.

Mayer, Martin. *The Fed*. New York: Penguin Group, 2002.

Meltzer, Allan. *A History of The Federal Reserve Volume 1:1913-1951*, Chicago: The University of Chicago Press, 2003.

Menard, Scott. *Applied Logistic Regression Analysis*, California: Sage Publications, 2002.

New York Stock Exchange.2005. *NYSE Overview Statistics*. Http;//www.nysedata.com/Factbook/ viewer_edition.asp?model=table&key=268&category=14. 28 February, 2005.

Sain, Stephen. October 27, 2004. *More Time Series Models*. Http://www-math.Cudenver.edu/~ssain/linmod. 12 May, 2005.
— 2005. *Identifying The Order of Differencing*. Http://www.duke.edu/~rnau/411arim2.htm. 12 May, 2005.

Salvatore, Dominick. *International Economics*, New York: John Wiley and Sons, 2001.

Salvatore, Dominick. *Managerial Economics in a Global Economy*, Ohio: Thomson South-Western, 2004.

Studenmund, A.H. *Using Econometrics: A Practical Guide*, Boston: Addison Wesley Longman, 2001.

The World Bank Group. 2004. *Data and Statistics*. Http://www.worldbank.org/data/copuntryclass/countryclass.html. 27 March, 2005.

The World Bank. 2005. *What is the World Bank* ?. Http://web.worldbank.org. 27 March, 2005.

The World Bank Group. 2004. *World Development Indicators*(*WDI*).

Http://www.worldbank.org/data/copuntryclass/countryclass.html. 27 March, 2005.

Transparency International. 2004. *Corruption Perceptions Index 2004.* Http://www. Transparency.org. 12 April, 2005.

Transparency International. 31 July, 1997. *Transparency International Publishes 1997 Corruption perception Index.*Http:www.transparency.de. 10 April, 2005.

Tyagi, Rahul. 2002. *How to Evaluate a Demand Planning and Forecasting Package What to Look for in a Forecasting Tool.* Http://www.keepmedia.com/jsp/article_detail_print.jsp. 27 February, 2005.

United States Government. 15 March, 2005. *Time Series Data Monthly Retail Sales and Seasonal Factors.* Http://www.census.gov/svsd/www/adseries.html 26 March, 2005.

United States Government. 1 September, 2004. *Advance monthly Retail Trade and Food Services Adjustment Factors for Seasonal and Other Variations of Monthly Estimates.* Http://www.census.gov/svsd/www/adfactor.html. 26 March, 2005.

United States Government. 29 May, 2003. *History.* Http://www.census.gov/ acsd/ www/history.html. 26 March, 2005.

United States Government. 22 December, 2003. *Milestones.* Http://permanent.access.gpo.gov/websites/www.commerce.gov/ Milestones.html. 19 February, 2005.

United States Government. 2004. *Mission, Vision and Values.* Http://www.bea.doc.gov/bea/about/mission.htm. 19 February 2005.

United States Government. 2005. *US Department of Labor; Bureau of Labor Statistics.*Http://www.bls.gov/home.htm. 13 March, 2005.

Quantitative Micro Software. *Eviews 5 User's Guide,* California: Quantitative Micro Software, 2004.

Yahoo. 2005. *Historical Prices.* Http://finance.yahoo.com. 26 March, 2005.

—2005. *ARIMA Modeling.* Http://facweb.furman.edu/~dstanford/forecast/ h1.htm. 14 May, 2005.

—2005. *Building a Seasonal ARIMA Model.* Http://www.hkbu.edu.hk/

~billhung/econ3600/application/app06/app06.html. 08 May, 2005.

—2005. *Criteria For Model Selection*. Http://facweb.furman.edu/~dstanford/forecast/h1.htm. 14 May, 2005.

—2005. *Forecasting Tools*. Http://facweb.furman.edu/~dstanford/forecast/h1.htm. 14 May, 2005.

— 30 September, 2004.*Historical Census Browser: Historical Background*. Http://fisher.lib.virginia.edu/collections/stats/histcensus/background/ 26 March, 2005.

—2005. *Moving Average Forecasting Models* Http://facweb.furman.edu/~dstanford/forecast/h1.htm. 14 May, 2005.

Index

G

H

I

L

M

N

O

P

Q

R

S

T

U

V

W